Henry
Ford

Industrialist

David Long

Cavendish Square
New York

Published in 2017 by Cavendish Square Publishing, LLC
243 5th Avenue, Suite 136, New York, NY 10016

First Edition

Website: cavendishsq.com

CPSIA Compliance Information: Batch #CS16CSQ

All websites were available and accurate when this book was sent to press.

Library of Congress Cataloging-in-Publication Data

Names: Long, David, 1961-
Title: Henry Ford: Industrialist / David Long.
Description: New York : Cavendish Square Publishing, [2017] | Series: History makers | Includes bibliographical references and index.
Identifiers: LCCN 2016001279 (print) | LCCN 2016010770 (ebook) | ISBN 9781502619143 (library bound) | ISBN 9781502619150 (ebook)
Subjects: LCSH: Ford, Henry, 1863–1947. | Automobile industry and trade—United States—Biography. | Industrialists—United States—Biography.
Classification: LCC TL140.F6 L66 2017 (print) | LCC TL140.F6 (ebook) | DDC 338.7/629222092—dc23
LC record available at http://lccn.loc.gov/2016001279

Editorial Director: David McNamara
Editor: Renni Johnson
Copy Editor: Michele Suchomel-Casey
Art Director: Jeffrey Talbot
Designer: Stephanie Flecha
Production Assistant: Karol Szymczuk
Production Editor: Renni Johnson
Photo Research: J8 Media

Printed in the United States of America

Metric Conversion Chart		
1 inch = 2.54 centimeters	1 mile = 1.609 kilometers	1 ton = 0.907 metric tons
1 foot = 30.48 centimeters	1 square foot = 0.093 square meters	1 pound = 454 grams
1 yard = 0.914 meters	1 square mile = 2.59 square kilometers	1 ounce = 28 grams

Table of Contents

1 Giant

More than any individual before or since, Henry Ford (1863–1947) is remembered as the man who took an expensive contraption of doubtful utility, a device then little more than a rich man's unreliable plaything, and brilliantly recast it as the machine that would change the world.

I t has been said that all political careers end in failure, and perhaps the same is true in the highest echelons of industry.

In 1945, when Henry Ford finally relinquished control of the company he had founded, losses at the Ford Motor Company were

This photograph of Henry Ford was taken circa 1910, shortly after the release of his most successful vehicle, the Model T, which would make Ford a household name across America.

running at an astonishing $10 million ($131.9 million in 2016) a month and the bills were piling up at such a rate that at least one department was weighing invoices rather than counting them. By this time the **autocrat** was well into his eighties and very much against his wishes, was finally forced out by members of his own family. His rude defenestration was in part stage-managed by a government concerned with the fate of what had become the largest industrial complex on the planet.

For all its size and Henry Ford's genius as an innovator, the business was on its knees. It might even have collapsed completely had it not been for lucrative government contracts to build hundreds of thousands of aircraft, trucks, and jeeps for the long war against Germany and Japan. Given time, it would recover, but the founder was finished. Less than two years after being ousted, the man who put the world on wheels was dead. His final hours played out in the flickering light of oil lamps when a freak storm silenced the technologically advanced generators he had commissioned years before to power his home.

The reasons behind his removal were sound, and the company might indeed have perished had its creator remained at the helm. Yet today that same bitter, cantankerous, and lonely old man is lauded as one of the great pioneering spirits of the twentieth century, and he is widely and deservedly hailed as a rare and authentic genius of industry.

The title takes some explaining. After all, Henry Ford did not invent the motorcar. By 1896, when he had built his first primitive automobile in his backyard, the German Carl Benz's

Patent-Motorwagen was already a decade old, and around two dozen of them were chugging around the streets of Europe. Nor, for all the claims that continue to be made on his behalf, did Henry Ford invent the **assembly line** or even introduce **mass production** to the motor industry. That honor goes to a rival, Ransom Eli Olds, whose pioneering Oldsmobile Curved Dash first went on sale in 1901, several years before Henry Ford had anything similar available.

But far more than Olds and Benz, indeed more than any individual before or since, Henry Ford is remembered as the man who took an expensive contraption of doubtful utility, a device then little more than a rich man's unreliable plaything, and brilliantly recast it as the machine that would change the world. He almost single-handedly transformed the way motorcars were built and sold, combining the role of visionary and zealot with the determination, grit, and personal energy needed to see a dream through to completion.

Because of this, and in a business with more than its fair share of brilliant innovators and powerful magnates—among them André Citroën, Vincenzo Lancia, Louis Renault, Britain's William Morris, and Giovanni Agnelli of Fiat—Henry Ford still stands tall as the motor industry's greatest-ever **mogul**. How great? Within a year of the Model T's launch in 1908 the company behind it was responsible for half the cars built in continental America, and before long Henry Ford could say the same of the entire world.

Pre-Ford America had not even built its own taxicabs—for years New York's fleet was imported from France, at that time the world's largest manufacturer of cars—but by 1920 Ford's Rouge River component plant in Detroit was its own motor city, boasting its own docks, more than 27 miles of conveyors, 16 million square feet of floor space, and a workforce one hundred thousand strong.

This seems to have been an industry that produced more than its fair share of **egomaniacs**, among them Italy's inspired but flawed Enzo Ferrari, Ettore Bugatti in France, Ferdinand Porsche, and Britain's Walter Owen Bentley. But here, too, none of them came even close to rivaling Henry Ford. Already middle-aged when he hit the jackpot with the Model T, his forceful but contradictory character, incendiary opinions, and deeply unpleasant personality came close to destroying everything that he had spent his life creating.

It was Ford's personal spark of genius, however, that ignited the industry on which we have all come to depend. Following his death, no one felt it necessary to contradict the Detroit newspaper that ran the news on its front page under the banner headline, "The Father of the Automobile Dies."

Henry Ford came from nowhere: a Michigan farmer's son who rose from traditional, rural roots to become a multibillionaire. Historic wealth comparisons are notoriously difficult to calculate, but at his peak he might have been worth in excess of $150 billion at present values. He was also a ruthlessly single-minded autocrat who became a genuinely popular folk hero and an ardent **pacifist** who went on to inspire Adolf Hitler and Joseph Stalin—neither of them in a good way. Here was a chief who voluntarily chose to pay factory workers twice what his competitors were paying, yet who went on to wage a bitter, personal war against **trade unions**; a man who genuinely wished to improve the lot of the working poor, yet committed deliberate and repeated abuses of power and employed thugs to enforce his oppressive rules.

Of course, only the most naïve observer would expect an **industrialist** operating on such a scale to be *nice*, but Henry Ford was worse than most. Early photographs show him with a wry little half-smile and a positive twinkle in his eye, looking every bit the benign, avuncular **benefactor** he thought he was. But the reality is that he paid his men double knowing this was the only way they could afford to buy the cars he wanted to sell to them. It worked, too, so well that Henry Ford got back much of the money almost immediately, which he then used to bankroll his own private newspaper.

Published with the express purpose of campaigning against Jews, whom he blamed for all manner of world ills including female fashions and jazz, news of the *Dearborn Independent* traveled far and wide. Today Ford enjoys the dubious distinction of being the only American citizen mentioned by name in Hitler's autobiographical *Mein Kampf*.

That we forgive him for this, or at least turn a blind eye to it, comes down to one car, the aforementioned Model T. The celebrated "Tin Lizzie"—the nickname possibly derived from a racing version, which, though battered, was victorious—is the car that motorized America. A well-engineered, soundly built **utilitarian** machine that ordinary US citizens could afford to buy and run, it was also the best possible advertisement for Ford's

Model T cars line the curb of Main Street in Savanna, Illinois, in 1916. Like in other cities in the United States, Ford's Tin Lizzie was the vehicle of choice.

company and one that helped propagate his radical production-line techniques. It was a creation whose underlying philosophy can be said to have paved the way for the machine age, to have kick-started a second industrial revolution.

Among customers in America's rural hinterland, the Model T was widely admired because it was rugged, straightforward to repair, and easier to drive than most of its rivals. Thanks to what now looks like a uniquely thoughtful design, it turned out to be largely free of the quirks and pitfalls that early motorists had hitherto considered inevitable. It was also versatile, so tough that little truck and bus variants soon joined the many car and pickup versions plying the dusty roads of early twentieth-century America.

By 1914, Ford was building so many Model Ts that his company had become the largest in America. At its peak, one car came off the production line every ten seconds. Such was its ubiquity that years later, in *Cannery Row*, the novelist John Steinbeck was to suggest that "most babies of the period were conceived in Model T Fords and not a few were born in them." Inevitably, not everyone greeted its arrival with such enthusiasm. The FBI's J. Edgar Hoover, for example, denounced cars generally as what he called "camouflaged brothels," even before hearing that both John Herbert Dillinger and Clyde Barrow—two of the most famous bank robbers in American history—had written to Henry Ford personally to congratulate him for designing their favorite getaway car. Henry Ford's competitors were not too happy either, realizing very early on that this new one posed the deadliest possible challenge to their continued profitability.

The Model T challenged the way everyone had been designing and building cars since the early days of the first "horseless carriages"—which in most cases meant using craftsmen to build them as if they were just that, carriages. Horses still cast a very long shadow over the auto business in those early days. Ransom Olds claimed to have designed his first car because he hated the smell of the stable, and Ford famously dismissed the idea that market research had any value, saying that if he had asked the public what it wanted before designing the Model T the answer would have been "make us a faster horse."

Ford's Model T provided a new three-dimensional blueprint for the future. Or perhaps that should be *the* three-dimensional blueprint, since just about every competing **marque** in the United States and abroad faced the dawning realization that if they were to stand the slightest chance of surviving then they needed to learn the lessons of what quickly became known as "**Fordism**."

Yes: Fordism. Such was the impact of the man and his car that before long Ford had become not merely the leading agent for change in the auto industry but a one-man worldwide movement, an "ism." Fordism was the new term applied to the sort of highly industrialized and **standardized** form of mass production that lay behind the Model T's success. It was something manufacturers ignored at their peril. Some of them might have built faster cars, more expensive cars, or better-looking cars than the Model T, but none of them managed to build *more* cars than Henry Ford, nor did anyone succeed in changing the world in the way that he had.

This is why Henry Ford is a giant. What he achieved with the Model T was complex and multifaceted, but then as now it is startlingly easy to describe. He identified a huge potential demand for a relatively cheap mode of private transport. To meet this popular need, he conceived the right machine for the time. And

Workers assemble the flywheel-magneto ignition system for
the Model T at Highland Park in 1913.

Ford employees work on an assembly line of car bodies circa 1927 in Detroit.

in order to make a profit, he reorganized the entire manufacturing process to build cars as cheaply and as quickly as possible. He did this by standardizing parts, part sizes, and procedures; by separating manufacturing from planning and management; and by subdividing the tasks needed to assemble the cars.

From then on individual workers carried out small, specific tasks using components that were fitted to the **chassis** as it moved along the production line. Today the technique sounds obvious, but at the time it was a giant leap, and one that was genuinely transformational. Its implementation made Henry Ford not merely an industrial pioneer—arguably the greatest industrial pioneer of the twentieth century—but a revolutionary. Ford was the man who changed the world and the way we live our lives, the man who recognized that, as he put it, "the market for a low-priced car is unlimited." The man who worked out how best to build it and who promised nothing short of "a new world, a new heaven and a new earth."

2 Early Years

Ford was transfixed. "It was that engine that took me into automotive transportation," he later declared, and he used to draw visitors' attention to a photograph on his office wall of the self-same machine.

Like the British carmakers William Morris and Herbert Austin, Henry Ford came from traditional farming stock. He was born on July 30, 1863, in Wayne County, Michigan, to a father who had abandoned Ireland for America during the Great Famine and a mother of Dutch and Scandinavian origins. His beginnings were modest, although he took pains in later life to distance himself from the legend that he had sprung from nothing.

Henry Ford sits in his first automobile, the Ford Quadricycle, which was one of a kind.

In the introductory pages of *My Life and Work*, his ghostwritten autobiography, Ford was quick to dismiss the notion that "my parents were very poor and that the early days were hard ones." Admitting only that William and Mary Ford "were not rich but neither were they poor," his own belief was that by the standards of Michigan farmers generally "we were prosperous." In fact, they came to own several hundred productive acres, and so in time were certainly to be counted among the more successful of the cohort that had crossed the Atlantic from Ireland.

His personal recollections were suggestive of a happy, if hard-working, youth spent lifting potatoes and picking fruit with his five younger siblings. Always more practical than academic, young Henry started attending a local one-room school in his eighth year. He must have enjoyed some of it—years later he bought his old schoolmaster's house—but was never a great reader or writer. From early youth onward, he appeared more interested in machinery than books and, according to his mother, Mary, he was "a born engineer."

As a youngster, he said, "my toys were all tools," some collected from around the farm and others that he made himself, including screwdrivers and files fashioned from knitting needles belonging to his mother. Impatient of theory but an extremely quick learner when it came to understanding anything mechanical, the loan of a watch belonging to a German farmhand was an opportunity to learn the basics of how timepieces functioned. An encounter on the road into the nearest town at around the same time was subsequently recalled as one of the real turning points in his life.

Traveling in a horse-drawn buggy with his father at the age of twelve, Henry Ford saw a vast but primitive steam-driven traction engine—"the first vehicle other than horsedrawn" that he had ever seen. As Ford himself remembered the occasion, he immediately jumped down from his father's side and was soon deep in conversation with the driver of this noisy behemoth. Determined to find out what it was, what it was used for and—most importantly—the mechanics of how the thing worked, Ford was delighted to find the driver was as keen to talk about the machine as he was to hear about it.

Eagerly absorbing the driver's words of wisdom, Ford was transfixed. "It was that engine that took me into automotive transportation," he later declared, and he used to draw visitors' attention to a photograph of the self-same machine on his office wall. The following day he returned to school and continued helping out on the farm in the evenings, but the die was cast. For Henry Ford the future lay in engineering rather than farming, about which—as he made clear in his autobiography—he always felt "considering the results, there was too much work." Thereafter he was always happier with a tool in his hand rather than a pen or pencil, fast becoming what his father described as "a lad with wheels in his head."

Soon after the serendipitous encounter with the steam engine, the gift of a watch of his own provided Ford with another opportunity to prove his ability and enthusiasm. Having rapidly removed the back of the case so that he could dismantle and then reassemble its delicate workings, before long he was making a few cents by mending clocks and watches for neighbors and family friends. As he approached sixteen, he finally managed to persuade his parents to let him leave the farm altogether and, after agreeing to lodge with an aunt, he walked the 8 miles to Detroit, where he hoped to train as an engineer.

His first job was as an apprentice building trams for the Michigan Car Company, but in less than a week he had been given his cards, possibly because his boyish enthusiasm tipped over into the kind of precociousness that many employers dislike in apprentices. From there he joined a firm that made bronze castings and then went on to the Detroit Dry Dock Engine Works, the city's largest shipbuilder. There he met an Englishman named Samuel Townsend, an individual whose contribution to the developing Ford narrative was to lend the eager young American some back issues of *World of Science*, a British publication that he read and reread at a gallop.

At this stage Ford displayed an almost Leonardo da Vinci type of mind, the sort that is excited by many different things, albeit mostly in the mechanical sphere. In particular, he was thrilled to read a piece by the late Dr. Nikolaus August Otto, the German inventor of the first practical four-stroke internal combustion engine. Also the son of a farmer, Otto's theories were highly advanced but far from mainstream. In these pioneering days of motorized transport, the smart money was still on steam rather than gasoline, with everyone from the US president to the New York Police Department choosing steam cars over any other kind.

That they did seems extraordinary now, but steam had a relatively long history, and few late nineteenth-century engineers saw petrol as a viable choice of fuel or had the courage to abandon what they knew for something not yet tried and tested. At its peak, America boasted as many as 180 steam-car makers, which built cars that were winning races as well as smashing international land-speed records long before any of the petrol-car makers had really managed to get into their stride.

Otto's ideas at least reminded engineers that the conventions of the steam engine did not necessarily have to be followed slavishly and that motorcars did not have to be simply scaled-down versions of the traction engine. Reading about this new and exciting kind of engine came as a revelation to Ford, Otto's contribution to *World of Science* providing him with a practical description of the intricacies of this novel source of motor force. It also contained—no less importantly—a detailed explanation of how a new generation of "silent" gas- or petrol-powered engines might actually be built.

From this point on Ford began to devour as much information as he could about Otto and his engines. Back issues of *World of Science* were soon supplemented by a subscription to *Scientific American*. Ford's autodidactic fervor and natural aptitude for machines very soon enabled him to exceed the mechanical knowledge of any of his peers, and much of the information he put to good use early on. For example, it was Ford who repaired one of the Detroit Eagle Iron Works' badly malfunctioning gas engines when it occurred to him that "no-one else in the town knew anything about them." This small triumph was followed by a short course in business administration, but then, at the age of twenty-one, he was back on his father's farm, where he was given around 80 acres on which to build a house and workshop.

In all, he spent nearly seven years on the farm, supplementing his income by fixing steam engines and, for much of the time one suspects, planning his next move. He married Clara Bryant after meeting her at a local New Year's Eve dance, and in 1888 he was offered a job as a $45 ($1,200 in 2015) per month machinist with the Edison Illuminating Company. Returning to Detroit, the couple rented a house at 58 Bagley Avenue, where he converted a small brick outhouse into a machine shop of his own.

Ford soon struck up a relationship with the famously industrious Thomas Alva Edison that was to prove useful and enduring. Including designs for the phonograph, the movie camera, and a workable type of electric lightbulb, Edison successfully filed nearly 1,100 US patents, making him the fourth most prolific inventor in history. The two remained good friends until Edison's death in 1931 but, while accepting promotions within the company (eventually to the post of chief engineer), Ford soon decided that, come what may, he was going to build a motorcar of his own. This meant he would have to leave his friend's employ.

Described years later by the English motoring journalist Leonard Setright as "unschooled and scientifically naïve," Ford was in many ways typical of the sort of men—and at this stage it was all men—who were drawn to the small but rapidly expanding

Legendary innovators Thomas Edison (*left*) and Henry Ford (*right*) became friends when Ford went to work for the inventor before starting his own company.

motor industry. At any one time scores of these would-be pioneers and innovators were working away in barns and workshops on both sides of the Atlantic. All were trying to make a horseless carriage that was better than its predecessor, and most would share some of their ideas in journals such as *World of Science* for others to copy, improve upon, or modify.

In the main they were mechanics and inventors—not scientists or entrepreneurs—enthusiasts and amateurs more interested in producing machines that worked than in theorizing about how efficient they were or establishing what they might sell for. They recognized that while reading was a fine place to start, the only real way to progress was to roll up their sleeves and actually build something. Trial and error was the best way forward.

Ford certainly saw things that way, and by Christmas Eve in 1893 he had succeeded in getting a crude petrol engine of his own design to run in fits and starts on Clara's kitchen table. It

Henry Ford made his first automobile in this workshop in 1890.

was far from the sort of machine a scientist or theoretician might have designed, but then it wasn't designed—it was built and working, and for Ford that was probably sufficient. As a farmer's son he would have inherited the sort of mentality that recognizes that if a machine works and keeps on working then that's plenty good enough, and this one did just fine.

With its single **cylinder** and a **flywheel** scavenged from a lathe, Ford's first engine seemed happy chugging along, so next he set about building a car. It too was going to be fairly crude, with no brakes, four wire-spoke bicycle wheels (where Carl Benz had been content with three), and a primitive two-cylinder engine mounted horizontally at the rear and running on ethanol. Completing it took more than two and a half years—all of it in Ford's spare time as he remained with Edison's company until August 1899—and when he finished it he found he had to tear down part of one wall of the workshop just to get it out.

Freed from its prison, the machine's maiden journey took place at 4 am on June 4, 1896. Mustering 4 **horsepower** and transmitting this to the rear wheels via 10 feet of bicycle chain, the "Quadricycle," as he called it, lacked a reverse gear and had only two forward ratios. Having insufficient torque, it tended to stick in first gear, giving it a speed of around 10 miles per hour rather than its theoretical "top" of 20. A single seater and weighing approximately 500 pounds, it was to cover around 1,000 miles with Ford at the tiller before being sold to a Detroiter named Charles Ainsley for a handsome $200 ($5,750 in 2015). Henry Ford happily pocketed the money. He was on his way.

3

If at First You Don't Succeed

Every single piece of these early automobiles had to be built from scratch or scavenged from elsewhere. Ford's cylinders were ingeniously wrought from a length of pipe taken from a steam engine, cut in half, and then bored out to the correct diameter. The driver's saddle similarly came from an old bicycle.

Ford immediately plowed the money from his first sale into a second Quadricycle, although his intention at this stage would probably have been to improve on

After a couple of failed start-ups, the Ford Motor Company would endure, through the Great Depression, after Henry Ford's death, and to present day.

the original rather than begin series production as part of a fledgling business.

The work was slow and painstaking and not simply because Ford had a day job. Without a component supply industry, every single piece of these early automobiles had to be built from scratch or scavenged from elsewhere. The cylinders for Ford's first car, for example, were ingeniously wrought from a length of pipe taken from a steam engine, cut in half, and then bored out to the correct diameter. The driver's saddle similarly came from an old bicycle, while what passed for the horn was no more than a domestic doorbell screwed on to the front. Nor at this stage was there any provision for a passenger, although the saddle on the first car was subsequently replaced by a more comfortable green leather toolbox-seat.

Aware of his creation's shortcomings, Ford spent some time tootling around his local streets before summoning up the courage to risk a longer drive out to his parents' farm. As in Europe, rural roads at this time posed a serious challenge for vehicles of any sort, being largely unpaved and thus far better suited to hoof than wheel. The Quadricycle suffered additionally because it was narrower than a farm cart. If the driver positioned it so that the wheels on one side ran along the ruts, the opposing pair would be several inches higher, forcing the vehicle to run at a tilt and making an already uncomfortable journey even more disconcerting. Coping with these real-world challenges was important, however. Town dwellers were relatively well provided for when it came to transport, and Ford recognized that in a country such as America this newfangled automobile, if it was to survive at all, would have to find buyers out in the boondocks—among people like his own folks.

Accordingly he set to work to figure out how to make the necessary improvements, and by the spring of 1898 the second Quadricycle was ready to roll. It differed from the first version in a number of small but significant ways. As well as conventional buggy seating, it now sported cycle wings over all four wheels, a pair of headlamps, and a drive chain relocated to the center of the rear axle rather than to the right-hand side. The finished result was evidently enough to impress Edison. He urged Ford on with the words, "That's the thing! Keep at it!" and encouraged its creator to seek backing from people wealthier than he.

One important early supporter was the powerful mayor of Detroit, William Cotter Maybury. Together with Michigan senator Thomas W. Palmer and real estate magnate William H. Murphy, he agreed to provide much of the finance Ford needed to leave Edison and establish his first company. Called the Detroit Automobile Company and incorporated in mid-August 1899, it was to last less than a year and a half before collapsing with debts of $86,000 (around $2 million in today's terms).

Despite the company's relatively short existence, as many as twenty vehicles were completed, including a half-ton delivery truck that was warmly received by a supportive local press despite a number of serious shortcomings. Where the Quadricycle was light, the little truck was heavy—too heavy. This made it too slow, in addition to which it was complicated to manufacture—meaning too expensive to make a profit—worryingly fragile, and awkward to maintain and repair. Not surprisingly customers were slow in coming forward, but Ford (who by this time was drawing a salary of $150 ($4,300 in 2015) a month) was in any case not interested in selling anything that fell short of his own exacting standards.

Naturally this infuriated some of his investors: men who were, on the whole, less interested in any future the automobile might have than in seeing a financial return. Most obviously they were discomfited by the thought of sitting on the sidelines watching Ford spend their money perfecting his own designs. Casting green-eyed glances at the rival concern run by Ransom Olds (whose Oldsmobile Curved Dash looked to be on the brink of paying handsome dividends to his backers), they made a move in January 1901 to block Ford and to wind up the company.

To Ford, what they did was more of a disappointment than a disaster. He refused to surrender and, with impressive self-confidence, concluded that his troubles had come from chasing profit in place of innovation. Quickly regrouping and with further backing from William Murphy, he had established a second small manufacturing company by November 1901.

The catalogue issued by the Detroit Automobile Company suggests a strong focus on practicality, its sales messages cleverly underscored by a detailed comparison of the relative costs to the customer of a vehicle pulled by a horse and one powered by gasoline. Using Ford's figures, and including purchase costs and running expenses, the horse and cart turned out to be 60 percent more expensive than the car over a period of five years. It was left to another manufacturer to point out the other big difference between the two options a few years later, when a 1905 advertisement declared, "You can kill a horse but not a Cadillac."

This new entity, called the Henry Ford Company, took a completely different direction, with its eponymous head choosing to pour his energies into building racing cars in the hope that the resulting publicity would eventually enable him to build other automobiles to sell.

Unfortunately this strategy meant that, once again, Ford soon found himself facing an office full of angry investors, shareholders stone-faced at the thought of funding further development of an (admittedly successful) 8.8-liter racing car and disappointed at the quality of the production version. For an expert opinion on the latter, William Murphy decided to call in Henry Leland, a supplier to Ransom Olds and a skilled machinist. Leland took one look at Ford's prototype and found fault with nearly everything.

In March 1902, Ford was persuaded to resign. He left the second company he had founded with a severance package of just $900 ($24,850 in 2016) and a commitment to himself "never again to put myself under orders." He also secured a promise that Murphy would not use the Ford name from then on, and under Leland the company was soon reincorporated as the Cadillac Automobile Company. This name, now regarded as quintessentially American, comes from Antoine Laumet de La Mothe, sieur de Cadillac, the seventeenth-century French explorer who founded the city of Detroit and whose coat of arms is still shown on the

Henry Ford built the *999* racer engine in 1902. In 1903, Barney Oldfield won the Winton Bullet with this vehicle. Henry Ford drove it on Lake St. Clair and broke the land speed record at 91 miles per hour.

hood of every car built by the company. (Leland, curiously, was also the inventor of the world's first mechanical hair clippers.)

Ford, however, was far from finished with racing cars. A great devotee of the notion that speed sells cars, he went on to build two more, known as the *Arrow* and the *999*. Both were crude but effective giants, fearsome 18.9-liter locomotives that successfully smashed a number of speed records, one of them managing to cover a mile at an average speed of 91.37 miles per hour across the frozen surface of Michigan's great Lake St. Clair. The sight of this must have been impressive, but in truth, with only four cylinders apiece and lacking suspension, bodywork, proper steering, and a differential to enable the wheels to turn at different speeds, neither of the giants seemed to offer much beyond great personal danger to the pilots and some potential to grab the headlines.

Of course it is possible that at the time, for Henry Ford, the publicity these great machines garnered was reward enough. But even so, with two relatively high-profile company failures to his name, 1902 could well have spelled the end to his motor industry career. If this was to be so then maybe going out in a blaze of glory might have been preferable to Ford, rather than quietly fizzling out in the usual way of so many underfunded tinkerers and dreamers—but actually he was far from beaten.

Before long another investor appeared on the horizon in the person of Alexander Malcomson, a wily and energetic Scottish émigré who had amassed a fortune dealing in coal. ("Hotter than sunshine" was his company slogan.) The two men had first met while Ford was at Edison, and Malcomson was now persuaded to form a modestly funded partnership to develop an entirely new road-going automobile. To assist in drawing up the design, Ford employed his first really significant associate, a skilled draftsman by the name of Childe Harold Wills.

The *Arrow* racer, another of Henry Ford's experiments, is driven by Barney Oldfield, a legendary race-car driver of the era.

Moonlighting for Ford, Wills had earlier helped shape the *Arrow* and *999*, and in late 1902 he joined the payroll of the new partnership at an agreed wage of $15 a week ($414 in 2015). What was to become the new Ford Motor Company was finally on its way.

With a background in toolmaking, and an educated interest in chemistry and **metallurgy**, Wills had hoped to become a cartoonist, but in his new role he could see that he was able to fill in some important gaps in his employer's knowledge. He knew far more about metal than the self-taught Ford ever did, and he could also read a blueprint, which his boss never managed to do. Basing it on Ford's signature, he was also responsible for creating the flowing lettering that still graces the blue oval badge featured on every Ford car.

From day one, Wills became, in effect, the company's chief engineer, although Ford never called him any such thing. As far as Ford was concerned, you just worked for Ford, and for decades no one in the company was given a title. Ford had a knack for recognizing genuine talent when it came his way, however, and keen to keep Wills on board, he made a deal agreeing to pay the young man 10 percent of whatever he, Ford, earned in addition to the $15 a week basic salary.

It was a deal that one day was to cost the Ford Motor Company many millions, but in 1902 all that lay in the future. For now there was precious little money for anyone or anything, just a man with some ideas and another man who was capable of putting them down on paper.

4 The First Fords

> *The company's entire financial reserves were down to just $223.63. Just in time the Model A went to a Chicago dentist, Dr. E. Pfennig, who paid $850, thereby paving the way for one of the great American dreams to unfold.*

W hile they had been working on the great 18.9-liter racing cars, money had been so tight that in the winter months Ford and Wills would reportedly break off from work every half an hour or so, pull on boxing gloves, and spar to keep warm. Fortunately by early 1903 things were

Though not as successful as the later Model T, the 1903 Model A was the start of the Ford Motor Company legacy.

on a better footing, and in pretty short order the two men had their first car ready for inspection. Another two-cylinder model, producing 8 horsepower from its 1.6 liters, this became the first car ever sold under the Ford brand. Appropriately named the Model A, the plan was to sell it for around $750 (about $200,000 in 2015), or about the same as the rival Cadillac.

In June 1903 the partnership of Ford and Malcomson was officially renamed the Ford Motor Company, but it was July before that first car was sold, by which time the company's entire financial reserves were down to just $223.63 ($5,950 in 2015). Just in time the Model A went to a Chicago dentist, Dr. E. Pfennig. He paid $850 ($22,600 in 2015) for the privilege of rescuing Henry Ford from his third corporate collapse, thereby paving the way for one of the great American dreams to unfold.

Almost simultaneously the company received deposits totaling $470 ($12,500 in 2015) for two more cars, and over the coming weeks and months many more followed, so that by April 1904 an impressive 658 cars had been ordered, built, and sold.

Now properly in business, Ford was very much the boss and Malcomson seemed prepared to take a back seat. It is important not to underestimate the role of Wills in the enterprise, however. Far from being a mere draftsman, he was to play a crucially important part in the development of all the early Fords. From the Model A right through to the end-of-the-rainbow golden-egg-laying goose that was the Model T, his fingerprints can be found on every car that left the factory.

For example, in later life Ford liked to claim that he had decided to use **vanadium steel** alloy (to lighten and strengthen his cars) after finding a piece of valve made of the stuff in the wreckage of a crashed French race car. In fact, it seems far more likely that the decision was jointly made with Wills, a man whose expertise in metallurgy Ford respected and who helped Ford find a reliable source of the metal when the giant Carnegie steelworks was unable to provide it.

Credit for this should also go to John Wandersee. Initially employed to sweep the workshop floor, it was he who perfected the high-temperature processes needed to make the alloy and who established at Ford a series of advanced metallurgical laboratories, which for many years were without equal anywhere in the United States. Similarly, while Wills could not claim to have invented the **epicyclic** or planetary gearbox—neither could Ford, as many rivals used something similar—it was certainly Wills who improved it to a point where for years the company was able to rely on his design to the exclusion of all others.

Of the three cars sold in July 1903, only the third one has survived: a red "Rear Entry Tonneau." Having had a mere five owners in more than 110 years—at least one of whom took it to Europe—it was finally bought back by the Ford family. It sits on a 72-inch wheelbase and weighs about 1,250 pounds. Its design is both compact and attractive. Reading the first road test, which appeared in the August 1903 issue of *Cycle & Automobile Trade Journal*, one can well believe that 1,700 buyers paid their

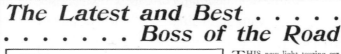

The Latest and Best . . . . .
. . . . Boss of the Road

THIS new light touring car fills the demand for an automobile between a runabout and a heavy touring car.

It is positively the most perfect machine on the market, having overcome all drawbacks such as smell, noise, jolt, etc., common to all other makes of Auto Carriages.

It is so simple that a boy of 15 can run it.

For beauty of finish it is unequaled—and we promise

IMMEDIATE DELIVERY

THE FORDMOBILE $850
. . . with detachable tonneau . . .

We haven't space enough to enter into its mechanical detail, but if you are interested in the NEWEST and MOST ADVANCED AUTO manufactured to-day write us for particulars.

FORD MOTOR CO.
692 MACK AVENUE   *DETROIT, MICH.*

Ford believed in making vehicles universal in both cost and ease of use. An advertisement for the Ford Motor Company's first vehicle states, "It is so simple that a boy of 15 can run it."

deposits, even if some historians now insist that no more than seven hundred Model As were ever built:

> *When in motion there is a light purring of the gear to be heard if one listens for it; there is absolutely no vibration to be felt; the riding is perfectly smooth and agreeable.*
>
> *The wagon is, of course, under entire control, and is extremely handy in a crowded street, and, taken all in all, this latest of American wagons offered leaves very little indeed to be desired.*

There will undoubtedly be advances in the art, but there will never be any wagon much more comfortable for its passengers than the Ford, and the machine work is excellent, everything being finished and secured in a workmanlike manner. The Ford Company finishes the bodies itself, and the external appearance is extremely good.

As money from Model A sales rolled in, a new factory was built at the junction of Beaubien and Piquette Avenues. By April 1905, the company had more than three hundred employees and was producing an average of twenty-five cars a day. It should be said, however, that even this new factory was really little more than an assembly plant. In common with its competitors, Ford still bought in components rather than making them, including engines and transmissions from John and Horace Dodge, who were yet to begin manufacturing cars of their own. Completed bodies were bought from the C.R. & J.C. Wilson Carriage Company—an operation that still exists and, under the name Fisher Body, forms part of General Motors—and wheels from the Prudden Company. Rubber tires were also bought in (we shall revisit this highly contentious aspect of production later).

Before long a new Model B joined the lineup, boasting a much large, 4.5-liter, four-cylinder engine. In quick succession it was joined by a 6.7-liter Model K as well as a range of smaller cars—no one called them economy models then—in the form of the N, R, and S, which shared the same 2.5-liter "four." By no

Henry Ford drives what he called an "automobile plow," an early tractor powered by his 1904 Model B engine, on one of his farms.

means were all of them successful, but by 1906 production was climbing to one hundred cars a day and Henry Ford could boast that he had built more cars that year than any other manufacturer. For such a young company it was a remarkable achievement—and one that was to be repeated every year for the next two decades.

The Ford Motor Company had become highly profitable, but there was friction. Malcomson had originally invested $28,000 ($745,000 in 2015) in the company and had more than doubled his return thanks to a 25.5 percent share of the company, which in the first year alone would have paid more than $60,000 ($1.6 million in 2015) in dividend payments.

Even so, he was eager to see profits rise further, and to this end he suggested to Ford that they push further upmarket. He argued that the future lay in luxury cars such as the Model B and Model K. But Ford took very much the opposing view, and when Malcomson formed his own short-lived luxury marque (trading as Aerocar) to prove the point, he was successfully maneuvered out of the company on the grounds that he was setting himself up as a rival.

It was an important victory for Ford. With Malcomson receiving $175,000 ($4.7 million in 2015) for his shares, it was also one that marked the beginning of the long process by which Henry Ford was gradually to buy back control of both his cars and his company.

With Malcomson out of the picture, Ford felt free to concentrate on his smaller, more affordable designs. These were the kinds of cars he was generally more drawn to and with which—in Europe at least—the company is still most closely associated. When the Model A was discontinued in late 1904, it had been replaced by the AC, with its only slightly larger engine, and then the C, which used the same 2.0-liter engine but had a vertical radiator. For the boy with wheels in his head, cars like these were heartland vehicles—cars that ordinary people could see themselves owning. This could never be said for the aforementioned Model B, which, for all its additional power (24 horsepower), was priced at well over double that of the best-selling Model A.

Precisely how many Model Bs eventually sold is not known, but at $2,000 ($53,000 in 2015) the figure is unlikely to be high. This, and the fate of Malcomson's Aerocar company—which lasted less than three years before being taken over—would appear to bear out Ford's belief that future success lay in building cars for the widest possible ownership. For a while he insisted that dealers take one of the even more expensive Model Ks each time they placed an order, but even with this ruse the company managed to shift less than one a day. Ford killed it off after two seasons and refused even to consider building another six-cylinder car until 1941.

Looking back, it is possible he disliked the car even more than the dealers did, and the public was certainly unconvinced.

Fortunately, the firm's smaller cars were doing much better business, especially the Model F, a two-cylinder machine derived from the C, and the Model N, which at just $600 ($16,000 in 2015) was even cheaper despite having an additional two cylinders. Admittedly it was only a two-seater, but for Ford it was also something of a landmark design. This was the first Ford production car to make use of the aforementioned lighter, stronger vanadium steel—indeed, it was the first production car to do so in the whole of America.

Sourcing the material from a small refinery in Canton, Ohio, which was prepared to risk the much higher temperatures needed to make the alloy, Ford later claimed to have taken the first ever delivery of American-made vanadium steel. For a number of

Overshadowed by the Model T, the preceding Model N of 1906 had a similar design and affordable price. The Model N could achieve a maximum speed of 40 mph and consumed fuel at 20 mpg.

A couple is seated behind their Model N Roadster.

years thereafter, the only cars in the world making use of the material were thus at opposite ends of the spectrum—a handful of expensive French luxury marques and the Ford Motor Company.

To many buyers this may have been a minor technicality, an invisible refinement even if it was one that brought a huge increase in tensile strength. But visible or not, the car quickly proved its worth by selling enormously well, thereby vindicating Ford's decision to remove Malcomson and to start thinking **mass-market**. By concentrating on the affordable Model N, the company was soon selling nearly five times as many cars as in its best ever year. A total of 8,243 sales in 1907 brought in a staggering $4,701,298 ($120.6 million in 2015) and for the first time produced an annual profit in excess of a million dollars.

The Model N proved something else as well: that innovation could be affordable. As an idea it was something that mattered a great deal to Henry Ford, and it was something he was soon to demonstrate even more brilliantly with his immortal Model T.

On the license plate: DEMONSTRATION 2-385-19 N.Y. 19

5 The Universal Car

> *With the Model T the intuitive engineer in Henry Ford set out to do no more than create a durable motor car of extreme utility. This was to be a car of real and practical value to the sort of people he had grown up alongside and understood best, a machine that people would buy and rely on.*

Work on what Ford described as his "universal car" properly began in 1906 when a small section on the third floor of the noisy Piquette Avenue factory was screened off and set aside for a small design team to engage

Henry Ford stands by a Model T, the automobile that changed the world.

A newspaper advertisement for the Ford Model T, circa 1909, details the car's parts and makeup, including the four-cylinder engine, vanadium steel, and light weight at 1,200 pounds. With a price of $850, it cost hundreds of dollars less than competitors' vehicles, and the ad states, "We make no apologies for the price."

in what in current business jargon might be termed "blue-sky thinking." Ford called the project "a completely new job," and the team was made up of Ford himself—moving between his mother's old rocking chair and a blackboard—Harold Wills, Ed "Spider" Huff, a Hungarian engineer named József Galamb, and a Danish woodworker named Charles E. Sorensen.

The initial ideas necessarily came from the man in the rocking chair, the remaining members of the team being there largely to interpret and make possible whatever was subsequently scrawled on the blackboard. Sorensen, for example, was adept at making three-dimensional wooden models to compensate for

This Ford Motor Company advertisement boasts of the motor's design and the car's affordability.

Ford's difficulty when it came to visualizing things from a simple sketch. A skilled mechanic who had worked alongside Ford for years, Spider's task was figuring out the electrics, while Galamb, as a trained engineer, designed many of the car's smaller components.

It has been said many times that, having never forsaken his farm-boy roots, the intuitive engineer in Henry Ford set out to do no more than create a durable motor car of extreme utility. This was to be a car of real and practical value to the sort of people he had grown up alongside and understood best, a machine that people would buy and rely on. But we now know that the Model T was going to be much more than this, and with hindsight it is hard to overstate its significance.

Its speed, simplicity, and strength meant that the Model T represented personal freedom for the people who bought it. At the same time, a commitment to make it truly affordable—indeed increasingly affordable—meant that this new car of Ford's actually proclaimed democracy.

Populism of this kind was almost unheard of at the time, but Ford was explicit. He wanted to build "a motor car for the great multitude," one that would be:

> *large enough for the family, but small enough for the individual to run and care for. It will be constructed of the best materials, by the best men to be hired, after the simplest designs that*

modern engineering can devise. But it will be so low in price that no man making a good salary will be unable to own one—and enjoy with his family the blessing of hours of pleasure in God's great open spaces.

A fine speech; but what marks it out from mere rhetoric is that by 1908 the words were starting to become reality.

The firm's twentieth design over a five-year period, the Model T, built on its predecessors but in almost every regard was more than just the culmination of what Ford had learned building and selling Models A through S. It was an entirely new development rather than simply the next iteration—more a giant leap forward than the next step.

With the Model T, Ford managed to achieve two extraordinarily significant objectives. First, designed to be efficiently manufactured and yet reliable and user friendly—attributes we take for granted today but which a hundred years ago were genuinely revolutionary—it was a car that any able-bodied adults with a modicum of skill could drive themselves. Second, it was engineered in such a way that it could be repaired without calling on a specialist motor mechanic or returning it to the factory. This marked it out from the rest in an industry where, for example, a spokesman for Daimler-Benz had once declared that the market for motor cars would always be limited to around a thousand because it would never be possible to train sufficient chauffeurs.

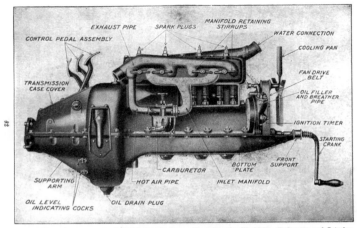

Fig. 8.—Valve Side of the Ford Model T Unit Power Plant Showing Manifolds, Carburetor and Interior of One of the Valve Spring Chambers.

A schematic of a 1917 Model T part shows manifolds, the carburetor, and the inside of one of the valve spring chambers.

It was, in short, a car for the people. It was also the car that would make Henry Ford very famous and very, very rich, and would go on to transform the face of America and eventually the world. The very notion of a "people's car" was wholly new at this time, and in truth it came as much from Ford's populist instincts as from a certain resentment that was becoming evident in his personality. As Robert Lacey observed in his magisterial 1980s biography, *Ford: The Men and the Machine*, Ford was a man who "resented the rich and fat's monopoly on the good life" and who had a "generous, almost didactic impulse to share the joy of machines with the world." Destined to remain in production for nearly two decades, the Model T was the happy result.

At its heart was an all-new engine, a 2.9-liter side-valve "four" constructed quite differently from the engines on which the industry had been relying up to this point. Traditionally, a cast-iron cylinder block was fixed on to an aluminum crankcase, with each cylinder cast separately and then bolted together. In a stroke of genius, Ford recognized that making this in a single, complex casting would greatly simplify both the manufacturing and the assembly processes.

He also introduced the now universal concept of using a simple detachable cylinder head instead of the conventional fixed one, and also of mounting the gearbox in a single unit with the engine. This meant that the mechanical heart of the car could be neatly dropped into the chassis frame in one piece, thereby minimizing the weight, complexity, and expense of manufacturing.

Simplifying things in this way produced a finished product that was both tough and relatively light thanks to its steel alloy construction. But the Model T incorporated numerous other innovations as well, many of which—once adopted by an industry initially skeptical of what the farm boy was up to—were to set the standard for many years to come.

Modifying a heavy and heavily insulated flywheel with copper coils and magnets, Spider produced the sparks for the cylinders. This was the first time **magnetos** had ever been fitted to low-priced cars, which hitherto had used dry cell batteries to fire the cylinders. For Ford it was an important refinement. Like the investor and philanthropist Warren Buffet years later, he never confused price with value: "Price is what you pay. Value is what

Workers on an assembly line, circa 1914, construct the engine of a Model T.

you get." Offering at low price what previously had only been available at a high price was to be a crucial part of the guiding philosophy behind the Model T.

At the same time Wills came up with a new design of epicyclic gearbox, one that meant the car could be operated using three pedals: one for braking, one for forward motion, and a third for reverse. This sounds simple on paper but it can be extremely confusing for the modern driver, used as we are to accelerator, brake, and clutch, and an increasingly diverse range of sophisticated automatics. But in its time it worked superbly, and in a world where potholes were both deep and plentiful, the ability to switch straight from forward to reverse and back again reduced the chances of a motorist becoming bogged down.

Critical to the car's success, however, was that it should be "universal." This meant that the car should sell globally, an ambition Ford emphasized by arranging for the car's public debut in November 1908 to take place not in Detroit or even Washington or New York, but at Olympia in West London. (In a useful publicity coup aimed at European buyers, the Model T also became the first car ever to scale Ben Nevis.) The term also indicated, in Ford's own memorable phrase, that it should eventually be possible to produce it "just like one pin is like another pin when it comes from the pin factory." As the company was soon to find out, however, achieving this smooth but important transition from craft manufacture to mass production was far from straightforward.

With the Model N the company had talked of building ten thousdand cars a year but struggled to achieve it. Initially it looked like a struggle for the Model T as well, a target price of $600 ($16,000 in 2015) looking hopelessly optimistic when it actually went on sale. In its first year the cost was nearer to $850 ($22,600 in 2015)—equivalent to a high school teacher's annual salary at the time—and then $950 ($25,300 in 2015) the following year. It was easy to talk of men "making 40,000 cylinders, 10,000 engines, 40,000 wheels, 20,000 axles, 10,000 bodies, 10,000 of every part that goes into the car" in a single year, but no one

Model Ts line up outside of the Highland Park plant in October 1913. Due to standardized parts and efficient assembly line manufacturing, Ford was able to out-manufacture his competitors.

had managed it yet, and that included Henry Ford. He was in a jam: building and selling more might reduce the price, maybe even to $600, but how to sell more?

Another man might have lost his nerve and watered down the plan or maybe even abandoned it altogether, but Ford took a radically different approach. He decided to change the way the car was built rather than changing and cheapening the car. Instead of diluting the quality of what he was building, he planned to improve the quality and quantity of the build, focusing on his company's new Highland Park factory, a bespoke, state-of-the-art facility on a 60-acre greenfield site that he opened in 1910.

Situated a few miles north of Dearborn, the plant was magnificent, its thousands of windowpanes earning it the nickname "Crystal Palace." It was also huge: four stories high, 865 feet long, and with nearly 750,000 square feet of floor space for its more than eight thousand machines. It was to become the birthplace of the first fully mechanized mass-production techniques in the automobile industry.

In April 1913 a moving conveyor belt was introduced in a bid to speed up the production of Spider's clever flywheel magneto. It worked brilliantly. As a further test, a temporary system was rigged up to haul individual chassis frames through the plant using a simple rope and windlass system. This worked too, despite being somewhat cumbersome, and reduced the time needed to make an entire car from just under twelve and a half hours to around six. This was slashed even further (with chassis assembly taking a little over one and a half hours) when the experimental

Factory employees work on the bodies of Model Ts in 1915, stuffing upholstery into the seats.

Heath Robinson arrangement was replaced by a proper moving track assembly line.

Within eighteen months, every major component of the Model T was being built on these moving lines, and with the factory effectively beginning to function as a single machine, car production began to soar. In 1911 it took around seven thousand workers to produce some 78,000 Model Ts—which was impressive. A year later employee numbers had doubled, along with production. Then, following the wholesale introduction of moving assembly lines, production doubled yet again, despite a 10 percent reduction in the number of workers manning the machines.

Falling far behind, Ford's competitors were aghast at what they saw. Some, such as Oldsmobile cofounder Fred L. Smith, dismissed Highland Park as "nothing but an assemblage plant." Writing decades later, the historian Douglas Brinkley was much nearer the mark. Rather than running on diesel or steam, he said, this new factory was powered by its founder's ceaseless quest to "save time, money and manpower through further mechanization."

The rate at which completed cars rolled off the lines boggled visitors to Highland Park and gave rise to what remains one of the most famous sayings attributed to Henry Ford. "Any customer," he said, "can have a car painted any color that he likes so long as it's black." The reason had nothing to do with Ford's increasingly despotic, controlling nature, and certainly nothing to do with the Model T being such a basic car. Rather it was entirely down to the time taken to build the cars, which was accelerating week by week. Japan black enamel apparently dried faster than any other paint, and from 1914 to 1926 this made it the only paint able to keep pace with an integrated system capable of churning out a new car every ten seconds.

In the earlier years, indeed, black had not even been an option, and for several years customers could choose only grey, green, blue, or red depending on the body style selected. As for the car being basic, standard equipment had included only three oil lamps, two up front and one for the rear, but customers could pay extra for headlamps, a hood, horn, and speedometer. Anyone wanting more had only to turn to the latest copy of the Sears Roebuck catalogue, which at its peak had more than five thousand accessories with which proud owners could customize their vehicle.

Even so, reducing the time needed by dropping colors, and with it the manpower, meant that the unit cost of manufacturing at Ford began to tumble precipitately. This allowed Ford to offer customers the same car at a lower cost while still increasing his profit. With much of this revenue returned to the factory, a virtuous circle was created, enabling Ford to make the factory even more mechanized and efficient, and thus continue the downward cost trend. Soon it was possible to buy a Model T for $450 ($10,800 in 2016) not $950, an extraordinary development and one that didn't bottom out until 1923, by which time a Model T "tourer" could be bought new for as little as $260 ($3,600 in 2016).

As prices dropped sales soared. They did so far faster and probably further than anyone might have forecast. By 1914, some 250,000 Model Ts were being produced annually, a figure

The chauffeur of a British family drives their Ford Model T in Pakistan in 1914.

that eclipsed all of Ford's domestic competitors put together. By 1921, the Ford Motor Company—or more correctly the Model T, since the company produced nothing else—accounted for more than half of all new-car sales in the United States. By 1925, the company managed to build some two million cars in a single year, more than thirty-eight thousand of them every week, and at something under half the unit cost of a decade earlier.

This was a global production figure. Unsurprisingly, news of the car had been quick to travel and so had production. Big new Ford-owned factories had sprung up in Britain, France, and Germany; cars were also assembled in Argentina, Austria, Belgium, Brazil, Denmark, Italy, Mexico, Norway, Spain, and even Japan. The first of these overseas transplants was at Trafford Park in Manchester, which began assembling cars in October 1911

A traffic tower at the intersection of Michigan and Griswold oversees the crowded streets of Detroit, circa 1920. The low cost and rapid production of Ford vehicles meant more vehicles and more drivers.

using components sourced from Detroit. The experiment was a huge success and just as it had dominated its home market, so the Model T now began to do the same overseas. By 1919, a staggering 41 percent of new-car sales in Britain were accounted for by Model Ts.

Eventually the company went on to capture half of the entire global market, an achievement never again equaled. Remarkably this was accomplished without paying for any advertising anywhere in the world from 1917 right through until 1923. In this, Ford was doubtless helped by the tardy response of many would-be rivals. William Morris, for example, delayed the installation of moving lines at his Cowley plant near Oxford until 1929, with the result that it took another decade before, finally, it could make its famous boast to have built one million new cars.

Long before this, on May 26, 1927, Henry Ford had watched his fifteen millionth Model T roll off the assembly line at Highland Park and then climbed into it with his son Edsel and went for a spin. This shiny black coupé represented a really extraordinary personal and corporate achievement, and one that no other company in the world would match for nearly half a century.

When the record was finally broken in the 1970s, the honor went to Germany's Volkswagen. Its Beetle could scarcely have differed more from the Model T in terms of engineering, appearance, and performance; but it was heavily influenced by it. Created at the behest of a man who wanted his own "people's car inspired by the American model," it was the cherished dream of Henry Ford's most sinister admirer, Chancellor Adolf Hitler.

6 The Meaning of Mass Production

> *However good the Model T, the secret to Ford's success and his wealth lay not in the car at all but in his mastery of mass production. Even more than winning the Car of the Century, this is what makes him the most significant single figure in what has long been the largest manufacturing industry in the world.*

Ford was a wealthy man before the launch of the Model T, but the new car quickly made him a multimillionaire when these were as rare as multibillionaires are today. By 1919, he was able to buy out his few remaining stockholders.

Bodies are mounted onto Model Ts on an assembly line at Ford's factory in 1913.

The transaction cost him more than $100 million ($1.4 billion in 2016)—an immense sum, but a few years later he was offered $1 billion ($14.1 trillion in 2016) for the company and unhesitatingly turned it down.

It wasn't just the Model T that enabled him to do this, although it was by any measure an outstanding little car and one that fully deserved the accolade of "Car of the Century" bestowed on it in 1999. The selection for this was made by members of the public and then voted on by a panel of industry experts from around the world. Second place went to the BMC Mini followed by the Citroën DS, the Volkswagen Beetle, and its Porsche cousin, the 911.

The secret to Ford's massive wealth, however, lay not so much in the car as in his mastery of mass production. Even more than manufacturing the Car of the Century, this is what makes him the most significant single figure in what has long been the largest manufacturing industry in the world.

In 1903 Ford's workforce of approximately 125 men produced 1,700 cars in a year. Each of these was relatively expensive but included a reasonable profit margin so that initially at least his shareholders had little to complain about. In 1905 around 300 men were producing twenty-five cars a day, a figure that had quadrupled by the following year. This meant that by 1906 Ford was already America's largest car maker; but even this impressive output was to be dwarfed once manufacturing moved to Highland Park, where Henry Ford could put his new ideas into practice.

The introduction of moving assembly lines in August 1913 saw production jump from seventeen thousand cars to more than two hundred thousand a year. The following year the total was up to 308,162, and two years after that it was 734,811—the equivalent of more than five years' production for Willys Overland, the company's nearest rival. The peak came in 1923, when Ford's US operation turned out more than 1.8 million cars, meaning they were outselling Chevrolet by more than six to one. John D. Rockefeller of Standard Oil was prompted to describe Highland Park as "the industrial marvel of the age."

It is tempting to imagine that Ford achieved this by stripping out all variety and building nothing but the Model T, but this is far from accurate. It is true that the company abandoned all its other cars in favor of the Model T, that no significant changes were made to the design over its near-two-decade life, and that rationalizing and maximizing production was an important consideration for Ford. But customers still had a wide range of choice. Almost from day one the company offered five different body styles, ranging from a two-seater runabout to a seven-seat town car. All were Model Ts, but by no means were they identical. Nor indeed were they all cars: truck versions continued to be built and to sell for some while after production of the car ceased.

Even in supposedly "progressive" factories (Oldsmobile, for example, which had been mass-producing cars since 1901) manufacturing could be painfully slow. A report in *The Engineer* on Britain's Humber Works showed that four fitters working on a night and a day shift between them could just about manage to build two small engines a week. Four men and a foreman similarly required a full week to produce three gearboxes, while

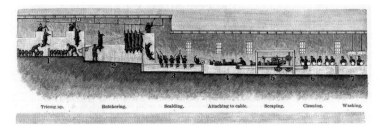

Tricing up. Butchering. Scalding. Attaching to cable. Scraping. Cleaning. Washing.

The efficient process of stockyards inspired Ford's assembly lines. This 1891 illustration details the stages of hog killing, from the pen to the cooling room.

another three were needed to build a single one of the company's larger 20-horsepower engines—assuming that they too were "continuously at work" for the entire week.

Ford was keen to move away from this kind of craft production. He claimed to have picked up many of his ideas from outside the industry. In particular, he singled out the Chicago meatpacking industry where "disassembly lines" processed vast numbers of pig and cow carcasses every day.

The work was horrible and labor intensive but also highly efficient, with thousands of animals passing through stockyards where each one could be slaughtered and butchered in a matter of minutes. The impressive speed with which this was achieved depended chiefly on the system, not the men doing it. The entire process from killing to chilling was broken down into individual, specialized tasks. Each worker was then responsible for just one task, be it hanging the doomed creature upside down, cutting its throat, scalding it, scraping, cleaning, gutting, de-larding it, and so forth.

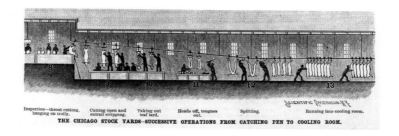

THE CHICAGO STOCK YARDS—SUCCESSIVE OPERATIONS FROM CATCHING PEN TO COOLING ROOM.

Convinced that "everything can always be done better than it is being done," Ford saw at once that it would be possible to divide up his own manufacturing processes in a similar fashion. He also realized that moving assembly lines could be used to bring the work to the workers rather than the other way around, thereby saving valuable time. Furthermore, if a man had only one precisely defined task to do instead of juggling several of them he could do it much better than before and much faster. Indeed, so long as the parts delivered to him were standardized, interchangeable, and correct, there seemed to be no reason why he should not be able to do it very fast indeed.

From early on at Highland Park the numbers bore this out beautifully. In 1914 it took thirteen thousand workers to make nearly 261,000 Ford cars, while the rest of America's auto industry needed more than five times that number to accomplish more or less the same. What's more, the mechanization that made this possible cost Ford virtually nothing. Each moving assembly line required only a simple belt running the length of the plant and an electric motor to move it along. The belt was fitted with pairs of metal plates that corresponded to the wheels on either side of the

Employees at the Ford Motor Company in Detroit head home for the day, circa 1930.

car, and as the completed car rolled out of the plant the belt would disappear beneath the floor and reappear back at the start of the line. These were things that could be acquired and installed easily, and at a capital cost to Ford of just $3,490 ($83,000 in 2016).

Even with such arrangements in place, however, Ford could see that further improvements were possible, and at every level of the four-story factory experimentation continued on an almost daily basis. With the introduction of new and improved lines, better conveyors, work slides, and rollways, scores of other ideas were wheeled out to see how well they worked.

Typical was the so-called "man-high line," which was introduced only three months after the first chain-driven conveyor. Designed to deliver all the parts at waist level, so the workers could repeat their assigned tasks without having to move their feet at all or bend down, it sounds almost **humanitarian**; but inevitably there were issues, not the least of which were boredom, dissatisfaction, and fatigue among the workforce.

Ford relished the opportunity to devise new and more efficient processes, and buyers were naturally pleased by lower prices, but the men who worked on the production line hated the system. The move to avoid anyone having to bend down to pick up a component was to do with saving time rather than minimizing discomfort and, far from recognizing or developing any skills a man might have, these new systems sought deliberately to de-skill the assembly process. While Ford naturally distanced himself from such an analysis—acknowledging only that he was putting "higher skill into planning, management and tool building"—the figures once again speak loudly. Staff turnover at Ford was soon running at record levels.

The workers, many of whom were immigrants and most of whom were indeed unskilled, earned $2.38 ($57 in 2016) for a nine-hour day doing work that was entirely unstimulating and that they did not enjoy. Unsurprisingly, many stuck at it for only a short period before seeking a better job elsewhere, so many that by 1913—in other regards Ford's *annus mirabilis*—the company found it had hired 963 workers over the course of twelve months to fill a hundred posts. Even those who didn't leave often failed to show up, and absenteeism regularly ran to around 10 percent of the workforce.

Ford's big problem was that instead of a hundred posts he had many thousands to fill, and demand for the cars meant the number was growing all the time. It didn't cost very much to train someone to do the work, but replicating the process at the scale of Highland Park's operation was completely unsustainable. Unable to ignore this, Ford tried to encourage the workforce to stay, using a variety of different incentives, including in-house medical care, after-hours clubs, children's playgrounds for families, and even bonuses. But nothing stemmed the outward flow, so eventually he proposed a far more radical solution: cutting the working day by one hour and more than doubling the pay to $5 ($120 in 2016) a day.

It was a move that looked altruistic but could just as readily be characterized as pragmatic, or even cynical. The *Wall Street Journal* accused Ford of treason against his class and of committing "economic blunders if not crimes." On Main Street, however, the

Immigrants employed at the Ford Motor Company attend English classes after work, sponsored by the Detroit YMCA, circa 1910.

move made Henry Ford a hero, even as cynics pointed out that much of the money would come straight back to Ford now that his workforce could afford to buy Model Ts of their own.

In this they were absolutely correct. Over the next three years company profits doubled from $30 million ($719 million in 2016) to $60 million ($1.3 billion in 2016), prompting Ford to observe that "the payment of five dollars a day for an eight-hour day was one of the finest cost-cutting moves we ever made."

Unfortunately the move was responsible for a dramatic change in the man's personality as well as his personal fortune, the great pouring forth of positive publicity persuading Ford that he was not merely right but almost papally infallible. Outwardly he looked the same, but as one biographer put it, behind "the gentle smile of a great benefactor" Henry Ford from then on became as ruthless as the great machines that built his cars.

Better wages improved staff morale and helped to boost productivity, but Ford wanted more. From this point forward he sought to manage his workers' lives not just in his factories but outside, too—a tall order in a place like Detroit, where brothels were rumored to outnumber churches and where there were any number of different ways for a man to spend his money.

Ford recognized that "high wages create large markets," but as a businessman he wanted wages to be spent on his cars rather than liquor, ladies, or gambling. As part of the $5 deal every worker committed not to spend it on alcohol. To oversee this injunction Ford created a new "Sociological Department" whose many hundreds of inspectors were authorized to snoop on the lives of Ford's employees.

Determined to ensure they did not indulge in anything that Ford himself considered "un-American," workers from Poland, Italy, Mexico, and the disintegrating empires of middle Europe were even warned against taking in lodgers. (Their increasingly despotic boss was convinced that, after alcohol, "dissension in the home is due to people other than the family being there.") Unfortunately such pronouncements soon became a routine part of life at the Ford Motor Company, as its founder and presiding genius began to view himself not simply as an engineer and manufacturer but as a philosopher with something new and important to share with the masses.

7 Pacifism and Anti-Semitism

> *Ford's declaration that "nations are silly and flags are silly too" was bound to get people's backs up. Similarly his insistence that he was going to stop flying the Stars and Stripes at his factory and replace it with another flag "which is being designed in my office right now" sounded just plain wrong to American ears.*

Henry Ford (*center, without a hat*) and members of the Peace Expedition stand on board the *Oscar II* on its way to Europe in February 1918, in the hopes of stopping World War I.

The most obvious conclusion is that Ford's extraordinary success was going to his head. Like any successful pioneer he had made mistakes, but these were chiefly in the auto industry, a world he knew and understood well. Now, having harnessed what he termed "the principles of power, accuracy, economy, system, continuity, speed and repetition"— and seen his Tin Lizzie become a global phenomenon—Ford the American folk hero stepped outside his familiar surroundings to set up his stall as a political figure and philosopher-prophet.

Ford was a self-professed pacifist, and ahead of America entering World War I he embarked on a particularly hubristic venture, chartering a liner called *Oscar II* in the belief that he might personally intervene to prevent Europe tearing itself to pieces. Seeking to fill the "peace ship" with what he termed a "people's delegation," Ford declared at the time that he would commit his entire fortune to the enterprise and "get the boys out of the trenches before Christmas." He would, he said, travel to Europe and stay there until he had defeated the spirit of militarism and prevented "murderous wasteful war in America and in the whole world."

Of the great and the good whom he had invited to join him on board, however, almost all felt able to decline. Only a handful accepted but even they failed to show up on the day that *Oscar II* was due to sail. Undeterred, Ford set off, but within days things began to fall apart.

The 1926 Ford transport plane nicknamed the "Tin Goose" had three engines and was used by both the military and civilians during World War I.

A Ford Tri-Motor Tin Goose is refueled in England in 1931.

When news reached the ship that President Woodrow Wilson had announced he was increasing the size of the army, presumably with a view to shipping troops to Europe, Ford retired to his cabin with the flu. When the ship docked at Oslo, he returned home almost immediately. Typical of the man, he refused to be daunted. Back in the United States, he admitted he "didn't get much peace but I learned that Russia is going to be a great market for tractors." Following the armistice, he signed a contract with the Soviets, who eventually purchased more than twenty-five thousand Fordsons, making Communist Russia the company's largest customer.

Had he left it at that he might have looked well intentioned if slightly naïve, but that wasn't Ford's way. A desire to keep America out of the war might somehow have been painted as patriotic, but his declaration that "nations are silly and flags are silly too" was bound to get people's backs up. Similarly, his insistence that he was going to stop flying the Stars and Stripes at his factory and replace it with another flag, "which is being designed in my office right now," sounded just plain wrong to American ears.

Admittedly, once the United States had entered the war, Ford threw his company behind the effort and thereafter worked with heroic effect, producing immense numbers of ambulances, trucks, and tanks, as well as thousands of sets of caterpillar tracks. Highland Park proved uniquely well placed to serve the war machine, and Ford agreed to produce the cylinders, as part of an enormous order from the government, for some twenty-six thousand Liberty aero engines.

It has been said that had these been manufactured in the conventional manner they might not have been ready in time for Hitler, let alone Kaiser Wilhelm; but just as they had done with the Model T, Wills and Ford soon devised a way of speeding up production and cutting costs.

Traditionally, aero engines had been made by machining them out of solid billets or finishing rough forgings that were then welded on to complex head assemblies. At Highland Park, however, where eleven thousand men and 500,000 square feet of the shop floor were given over to the project, the cylinders were made using welded steel tubing, which special machines then shaped to form the cylinder head complete with inlet and exhaust valve ports.

This was much faster and nearly 70 percent cheaper. The government rewarded Ford for his innovation with a contract to make all the cylinders as well as five thousand complete engines. Only four thousand were built before the war ended, but it was to be the start of something new and huge. A few years later Ford became the first company anywhere in the world to mass-produce aircraft and, from 1925 to 1933, it built some two hundred examples of its "Tin Goose," the Tri-Motor airliner.

The end of the war also saw another huge company plant nearing completion and a worrying development in Ford's personal crusading. At the new Rouge River complex in Dearborn, vast furnaces and forges—the largest in the world—were taking in ore and shipping finished components to the assembly lines at Highland Park. At the same time Ford was pouring money into

The Ford International Weekly

THE DEARBORN INDEPENDENT

One Dollar — Dearborn, Michigan, May 22, 1920 — Five Cents

The International Jew:
The World's Problem

"Among the distinguishing mental and moral traits of the Jews may be mentioned: distaste for hard or violent physical labor; a strong family sense and philoprogenitiveness; a marked religious instinct; the courage of the prophet and martyr rather than of the pioneer and soldier; remarkable power to survive in adverse environments, combined with great ability to retain racial solidarity; capacity for exploitation, both individual and social; shrewdness and astuteness in speculation and money matters generally; an Oriental love of display and a full appreciation of the power and pleasure of social position; a very high average of intellectual ability."

—The New International Encyclopedia.

THE Jew is again being singled out for critical attention throughout the world. His emergence in the financial, political and social spheres has been so complete and spectacular since the war, that his place, power and purpose in the world are being given a new scrutiny, much of it unfriendly. Persecution is not a new experience to the Jew, but intensive scrutiny of his nature and super-nationality is. He has suffered for more than 2,000 years from what may be called the instinctive anti-semitism of the other races, but this antagonism has never been intelligent nor has it been able to make itself intelligible. Nowadays, however, the Jew is being placed, as it were, under the microscope of economic observation that the reasons for his power, the reasons for his separateness, the reasons for his suffering may be defined and understood.

In Russia he is charged with being the source of Bolshevism, an accusation which is serious or not according to the circle in which it is made; we in America, hearing the fervid eloquence and perceiving the prophetic ardor of young Jewish apostles of social and industrial reform, can calmly estimate how it may be. In Germany he is charged with being the cause of the Empire's collapse and a very considerable literature has sprung up, bearing with it a mass of circumstantial evidence that gives the thinker pause. In England he is charged with being the real world ruler, who rules as a super-nation over the nations, rules by the power of gold, and who plays nation against nation for his own purposes, remaining himself discreetly in the background. In America it is pointed out to what extent the elder Jews of wealth and the younger Jews of ambition swarmed through the war organizations—principally those departments which dealt with the commercial and industrial business of war, and also the extent to which they have clung to the advantage which their experience as agents of the government gave them.

IN SIMPLE words, the question of the Jews has come to the fore, but like other questions which lend themselves to prejudice, efforts will be made to hush it up as impolitic for open discussion. If, however, experience has taught us anything it is that questions thus suppressed will sooner or later break out in undesirable and unprofitable forms.

The Jew is the world's enigma. Poor in his masses, he yet controls the world's finances. Scattered abroad without country or government, he yet presents a unity of race continuity which no other people has achieved. Living under legal disabilities in almost every land, he has become the power behind many a throne. There are

ancient prophecies to the effect that the Jew will return to his own land and from that center rule the world, though not until he has undergone an assault by the united nations of mankind.

The single description which will include a larger percentage of Jews than members of any other race is this: he is in business. It may be only gathering rags and selling them, but he is in business. From the sale of old clothes to the control of international trade and finance, the Jew is supremely gifted for business. More than any other race he exhibits a decided aversion to industrial employment, which he balances by an equally decided adaptability to trade. The Gentile boy works his way up, taking employment in the productive or technical departments; but the Jewish boy prefers to begin as messenger, salesman or clerk—anything—so long as it is connected with the commercial side of the business. An early Prussian census illustrates this characteristic: of a total population of 269,400, the Jews comprised six per cent or 16,164. Of these, 12,000 were traders and 4,164 were workmen. Of the Gentile population, the other 94 per cent, or 153,236 people, there were only 17,000 traders.

A MODERN census would show a large professional and literary class added to the traders, but no diminution of the percentage of traders and not much if any increase in the number of wage toilers. In America alone most of the big business, the trusts and the banks, the natural resources and the chief agricultural products, especially tobacco, cotton and sugar, are in the control of Jewish financiers or their agents. Jewish journalists are a large and powerful group here. "Large numbers of department stores are held by Jewish firms," says the Jewish Encyclopedia, and many if not most of them are run under Gentile names. Jews are the largest and most numerous landlords of residence property in the country. They are supreme in the theatrical world They absolutely control the circulations of publications throughout the country. Fewer than any race whose presence among us is noticeable, they receive daily an amount of favorable publicity which would be impossible did they not have the facilities for creating and distributing it themselves. Werner Sombart, in his "Jew and Modern Capitalism" says, "If the conditions in America continue to develop along the same lines as in the last generation, if the immigration statistics and the proportion of births among all the nationalities remain the same, our imagination may picture the United States of fifty or a hundred years hence as a land inhabited only by Slavs, Negroes and Jews, wherein the Jews will naturally occupy the position of

This article published in the *Dearborn Independent* on May 22, 1920, was the first in Henry Ford's seven-year publishing campaign against Jews. It even states, "Persecution is not a new experience for the Jew," and goes on to criticize the Jewish nation's character, culture, and ethics.

another enterprise, a newspaper called the *Dearborn Independent*, which he had acquired specifically to disseminate his increasingly toxic prejudices against Jews.

With no partners or shareholders to answer to, no banks to worry about, and no borrowings, Ford was free to say and do as he saw fit. He chose to use "Mr Ford's Page" in the paper as his principal mouthpiece. Typical outpourings included the charge that America's national debt was part of a Jewish plot to enslave Americans and that the financier Paul Warburg had emigrated from Germany to America expressly to create the Federal Reserve to destabilize the economy. Jews, said Ford, were an "international nation," something that gave them unfair advantages over Christian businessmen, who relied on their own individual talents to get ahead.

Ford's supporters dismiss such comments as mere symptoms of a Midwestern farmer's inherent distrust of big-city finance. As proof, they point to his boast that he made "cars not money" and stress the slightly comedic eccentricity of one who blamed Jews for post-war developments such as shorter skirts and the "abandoned sensuousness" of jazz.

Unfortunately they ignore the concerted way in which the newspaper railed against "the international Jew"—a sinister phrase familiar to any student of the Nazis' rise to power—and its enthusiastic support for such scurrilous and palpable forgeries as the *Protocols of the Learned Elders of Zion*. (The starting point for a thousand discredited conspiracy theories, on the basis of no evidence whatever, the Tsarist-era *Protocols* has been accepted by the credulous as a blueprint for a Jewish takeover of the world.)

Ford certainly didn't think his views were harmless or eccentric, and he worked hard to fuse what one might term his three great hates—Jews, war, and the unions—into a single, overarching conspiracy. The unions, he insisted, "are being organized by Jewish financiers [whose] object is to kill competition so as to reduce the income of the workers and eventually bring on war."

Adolf Hitler rarely put it any better, and indeed when the collected wisdom of "Mr Ford's Page" was republished in four volumes as *The International Jew*, copies soon found their way to Germany, where they sold well. The future Führer is known to have read their contents with interest, and at least one defendant in the post-war Nuremberg Trials also referred to the books in his defense. Specifically, Hitler Youth leader Baldur von Schirach claimed that *The International Jew* had made a deep impression on him and his friends in their youth and had influenced them in becoming **anti-Semitic**.

Hitler and Ford never met, but the American was mentioned by name in the second volume of *Mein Kampf*, and by 1922 it was reported (quite correctly) in the *New York Times* that Hitler kept a portrait of the great man in his party office. Here, too, Ford's supporters have argued that this respect was due more to his towering automotive achievements than his anti-Semitic philosophy, but clearly the two men shared a lot more than a desire to see the masses efficiently motorized.

Der Internationale Jude is a 1922–1924 German translation of Henry Ford's *The International Jew*, published in three volumes.

Where Hitler is concerned, we know where his belief about Jews led, but history sometimes falls silent on America's most notorious anti-Semite. He was not alone in his prejudices, of course. The celebrated aviator Charles Lindbergh was equally outspoken in attacking Jewish "ownership and influence in our motion pictures, our press, our radio and our government." Much like Ford, he also warned that "instead of agitating for war, the Jewish groups in this country should be opposing it in every possible way for they will be among the first to feel its consequences." Like Ford, Lindbergh was another curiously unsophisticated high achiever, his own sister-in-law describing him as a mechanic who, but for his solo flight across the Atlantic, "would now be in charge of a gasoline station on the outskirts of St. Louis."

But Ford went further. Spending money and energy turning an otherwise obscure weekly local newspaper into a national organ of poisonous propaganda, he also insisted it be stocked by all registered Ford dealers. Many reportedly paid for copies but then destroyed them rather than risk offending potential buyers. Where once he had committed his entire fortune to preventing conflict, he now seemed hell-bent on promoting it, finding a cause, inventing an antagonist, and doing all he could to foment discord.

Subtitling his four volumes "The World's Foremost Problem," Ford carefully built up a picture of cold-hearted Jewish manipulators, a race answering to none but themselves and seeking nothing short of world domination. The volumes sold depressingly well, but having sown the wind, Ford was soon reaping the whirlwind.

Jewish objections were joined by those representing powerful Christian interests and no fewer than three US presidents. Like Hitler, Ford found himself fighting a war on two fronts. On the one side, his company was finally beginning to face serious competition from rivals able at last to grasp what Ford had achieved with the now-aging Model T. On the other, in 1924 Ford was on the receiving end of a million-dollar libel suit filed by Aaron Sapiro, a lawyer and activist he had unwisely characterized as a kingpin in the malign, international Jewish cabal he had been warning the world about.

For a while he refused to change anything he said or did—"nothing is wrong with anything," to use his own hubristic phrase—but then in 1927 he suddenly closed the newspaper, settled the lawsuit with Sapiro, and issued a humiliating apology that is now a matter of public record. He read from the prepared statement:

> *I deem it my duty as an honourable man to make amends for the wrong done to the Jews as fellow-men and brothers, by asking their forgiveness for the harm that I have unintentionally committed, by retracting so far as lies within my power the offensive charges laid at their door.*

The speech was written by someone else and was wholly insincere. None of it altered how Ford felt. His private notebooks make this plain, and he still made the occasional outburst against Jews whenever his company faced hard times.

In 1938, on the occasion of his seventy-fifth birthday, he was also delighted to receive the Grand Service Cross of the Supreme Order of the German Eagle, a medal personally bestowed on him by the Führer. Because of this a Jewish boycott against Ford cars remained intact until the 1940s, eventually prompting Ford to repeat his apology. The company also made strenuous efforts to prevent further distribution of *The International Jew*, a publication now banned in Germany although pirate copies continue to circulate elsewhere.

8

Fordlandia: The Death of a Dream

Ford was already thinking about his next big idea. This was Brazil or, as his part of it was to become known, "Fordlandia." As outsized as the man himself, this latest project sprang from a desire on Ford's part to free himself from a monopoly in rubber, a monopoly owned and controlled by the British imperial interest in Malaya.

J ust as he had been slow to respond to his own "Jewish Question," Ford continued to ignore the fact that his beloved Model T was finally reaching the end of the road. It had enjoyed a phenomenally good run of nineteen years,

Today, abandoned and overgrown buildings are all that remain of Henry Ford's dream, Fordlandia.

and many millions had gone along for the ride. But Ford's policy of resisting all attempts by those around him to introduce even modest styling and engineering changes meant that the Model T was in danger of extinction.

Among those urging change on Ford were his son Edsel and Harold Wills. Edsel was always more interested in styling than his father, and Wills later recounted how on one occasion Ford was shown plans for a new Model T. This was lower, clearly better looking, and had numerous detail improvements, but Ford was so outraged that anyone should dare to tinker with his design that he ordered the prototype to be destroyed on the spot.

Eventually even he could see what was happening, however, and in May 1927 Ford finally shut down the production lines, aware at last that the car on which his empire had been founded was now at risk of causing it to collapse. World-beating in 1908, jolly good ten years later, and still almost good enough nearly a decade after that, it was starting to be embarrassed by its rivals. New competitors were springing up everywhere, and for the first time one of them was about to overtake Ford in terms of sales. With the American economy beginning to falter during one of several rehearsals for the coming Great Depression, new-car sales fell by nearly a million and Chevrolet's management woke up to find they had outsold their rivals at Ford by two hundred and fifty thousand.

Now in his mid-sixties, more dogmatic and dictatorial than ever and increasingly reluctant to embrace change, the reality for Ford was that he had nothing to offer in place of the once all-conquering Tin Lizzie.

When the US lines were shut down the final total for North American production was 15,007,033, to which must be added approximately 1.5 million produced overseas. Several customers reportedly bought multiple cars in the final few weeks, so sad were they to see it go, but Ford was nevertheless still forced to shutter twenty-three plants and lay off as many as sixty thousand men for the best part of a year. Desperate catch-up work began to design and retool the factories for a replacement.

Meanwhile, away from the suddenly silent assembly lines, Ford was already thinking about his next big idea. This was Brazil or, as his part of it was to become known, "Fordlandia." As outsized as the man himself, this latest project sprang from a desire on Ford's part to free himself from what had become a virtual global monopoly in rubber, a monopoly owned and controlled by the British imperial interest in Malaya.

The auto industry in America was consuming rubber at a phenomenal rate by the mid-1920s: an estimated three-quarters of a billion dollars' worth a year, with much of the bill landing on Ford's own desk. It wasn't just the expense that irked him, nor even the fact that his need for rubber—chiefly for tires but also for hoses, valves, and gaskets—was channeling money out of America to a foreign power.

Ford was no fan of the British or the empire, and he certainly didn't like being dependent on London for anything. His chief problem, however, was that by this stage he controlled every other raw material, literally owned every natural resource that went into the making of a car. Everything, that is, except the latex needed to make vulcanized rubber—and he didn't like it.

There had been talk of growing trees for latex in the Florida Everglades, and for a while Ford supported his friend Edison's attempt to produce "war rubber," a synthetic compound made from milkweed. But neither idea came to much. After a heated conversation with tire company boss Harvey Firestone, Ford had his secretary look into where might be the best place to grow his own trees. Ernest Liebold, Ford's adviser, declared the logical answer to be Liberia in West Africa but dismissed this on the grounds that the country was "composed entirely of Negroes whose mental and intellectual possibilities are quite low." Instead the two men settled on the Amazon. With more than 5 million acres in their sights, the die was cast.

Seeing this region of the world as one "uncorrupted by unions, politicians, Jews, lawyers, militarists, and New York bankers," Ford liked the plan enormously. The Brazilians were also keen, having lost the rubber monopoly to Southeast Asia nearly two decades earlier. But the project was to prove a painful and expensive failure. It cost Ford an estimated $1 billion in today's terms, and in nearly twenty years, Fordlandia produced not a single drop of latex for use in his cars. Eventually, the whole enterprise collapsed and was sold back to Brazil's government for a pittance.

Many of the worst problems arose because this ambitious scheme's administration depended on the same strange blend of paternalism and dictatorship that Ford had been practicing

A laborer slashes a tree to gather rubber on a Malaysian plantation, circa 1960.

back home in Michigan. To begin with, his plans seemed sound enough. Brazilians, Ford emphasized from the start, had the right to work as free men not slaves, and on learning that most rubber tappers earned less than 50 cents a day, he never doubted that he "would pay up to five dollars a day for a good worker."

In a similarly enlightened vein, he also determined that in creating Fordlandia the very best of America would be exported to Brazil. A film made at the time by Ford's friend Walt Disney demonstrated what he meant by this. It describes the creation of a model community designed to be self-sufficient in every detail. Besides modern factories and farms, the audience for *The Amazon Awakens* were told:

> *There are nonprofit stores and shops, where food and clothing are sold to the employees. There's modern road-building equipment, and 200 miles of roads have already been constructed to the plantation. The 5,000 inhabitants are provided with every means of making life in the jungle healthy, happy and comfortable. The workers' houses are clean and airy and offer a pleasant environment with modern conveniences.*

Unfortunately this was the best of America only as envisioned by Henry Ford. While snooping on his workforce (as his Sociological Department had been doing in Dearborn), in practice it meant Ford's managers exporting prohibition to the Amazon along with prefabricated houses and rules requiring the Brazilians—

free men or not—to refrain from doing anything that Ford personally disliked.

Soon there were even regulations constraining the workers' diet. Ford, the food faddist, insisted they eat unpolished rice and whole-wheat bread as well as peaches specially imported from Michigan: anything, it seemed, "to obviate any necessity of recourse to a native tropical diet." And there were more regulations, including an extraordinary ban on samba dancing (which, like jazz music, was considered too sensual). The Brazilians were encouraged to learn square dancing instead, the moves for which were imported from the Michigan suburbs along with curious homely wooden-framed buildings in which they were expected to live. The street names gave the game away: besides Main Street, Fordlandia boasted both a Hillside Avenue and a Riverside Avenue. Only nearby Palm Avenue seemed grudgingly to acknowledge the enclosing jungle. Ford's intrusive micromanagement of his workers' lives in this way very quickly backfired. Petty regulations strictly enforced were soon to be the cause of many complaints and eventually even riots.

Throughout Fordlandia there were practical problems, too.

Whatever accusations could be laid at the door of the British in Malaya, they were good at cultivating latex. By contrast, at Fordlandia, basic mistakes were made and then compounded by company men completely out of their depth. Ford had always despised experts and chose not to employ any in Brazil, so that across more than 2.5 million acres rubber trees were soon being planted in the wrong places, in the wrong soil, and at the wrong time of year. They were also planted at the incorrect density, something that hampered production by incubating the growth of myriad pests and deadly leaf blight in the already highly fecund atmosphere of the rain forest.

Many hundreds of workers also found ways to circumvent the absurd rules being imposed on them. Disliking Ford's diet, they disappeared into the forest in search of avocados, wild bananas, grapefruit, oranges, and lima beans. Ignoring his prohibition on alcohol, they made regular visits to the bars and bordellos, which soon proliferated around the boundary of Ford's private world. Others simply disappeared, presumably going back to their families once they had saved enough money to live for a few months without working. Unwilling to labor through the punishing dry season, when a rich variety of ticks, jiggers, blackflies, and ants could be relied on to bite more than ever, the prospect of returning home to tend one's own smallholding proved a far more attractive option.

Incredibly, Henry Ford chose not to set foot in the place even once, and in his absence his trusted manager—recalled now as a big man with a small brain—was not up to the job of holding everything together. A Norwegian ex-seaman, Einar Oxholm struggled from the word go and, following the death of three of his children from fever and a housekeeper who lost her arm to a river caiman, he failed to make what Ford's labor recruiter, David Riker, referred to as "365-day machines out of these people." He also drank.

For a long time reports sent back to Dearborn attempted to disguise what was going on, but eventually, in the absence of any latex, it was impossible to conceal the project's total failure. Even then, when the scale of the disaster had become apparent, Henry Ford was not prepared to visit or to admit publicly what had gone wrong. Instead a publicity campaign was launched to put a more positive spin on what was happening. Briefly it worked. In late December 1931 the *New York Times* gleefully reported how the motor mogul was spending "millions of dollars on the scientific growing of rubber. The settlement, once a waste, has been converted into a model city where high wages prevail."

The truth, however, was that the wages were still just a few cents a day and, far from the 6 billion pounds a year that had been forecast, there was no sign at all of the latex Ford needed to make his tires. Nor was there ever going to be. Even so, the more the project failed, the more its instigator sought to justify it on his own peculiar philosophical terms. Gradually the word "rubber" slipped out of the press releases, and in its place Ford personally and corporately began to speak of a civilizing mission.

However, even in this regard Fordlandia was a failure. The Middle America of Ford's youth was as welcome in the Amazon as his peculiar diet and no better suited to it. A neat and well-ordered community of straight roads, fenced front gardens, and clean living might have sounded fine in theory, but in practice, in the jungle, clapboard bungalows with asbestos and metal roofs

A local taps rubber from a tree in Central America in 1903.

(chosen by Michigan engineers to repel the sun) were, in the words of visiting priest A.B. Langlois, "hotter than the gates of hell."

Even had they proved fit for purpose, and had the diet been accepted along with the prohibition on alcohol and women and all the rest of it, it is hard to feel sorry about Fordlandia's failure. The whole episode now looks like an absurd neocolonial attempt to turn back the clock and to create a world like the one Henry Ford thought he could remember. It was almost as if, having shown the world what mass production and mass consumption could achieve, he wanted to put the genie back in the bottle and have nothing more to do with it.

He couldn't do that, of course; no one could. Instead he turned his back on Fordlandia and Brazil and hoped everyone would forget about it. In time they did, and a couple of years after Ford's death it was quietly disposed of. Today almost nothing remains beyond moldering bungalows, weed-strewn roads, and the shattered remains of collapsing barracks and factories.

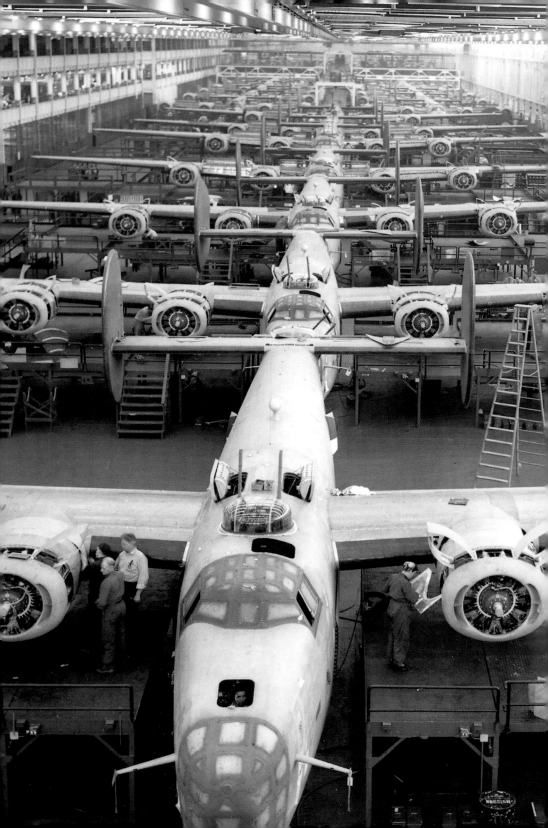

9

A Pacifist Rescued by War

The forces arrayed against Germany and Japan needed to tap into Ford's production expertise. Work began immediately on a new $60 million assembly line at Willow Run, just outside Detroit. The world's largest, at nearly a mile long, the end product was to be entire airplanes not merely engines—thousands of them.

enry Ford was sixty-four years old when he finally shut down the Model T assembly lines in 1927. Extremely rich and widely respected, had he retired along with his Tin Lizzie, he would have left the industry with his reputation as the world's great manufacturing genius largely unsullied.

Ford's B-24E Liberators were built for World War II on production lines at the Willow Run plant in Michigan.

He could have done so easily. His son Edsel had been appointed president of the company back in 1918, and sixty-four would have been a perfectly reasonable age for Ford to bow out. But although there were plenty of signs that the old man was beginning to lose his grip, Ford Senior felt he was far from done.

Henry Ford and his son, Edsel, a president of the company, pose in front of one of the unsung models that followed the Model T.

The time taken to design the Model A, the replacement to the Model T, and get it into full production had cost the company around a billion dollars, as well as the Ford Company's long-standing, much-prized market leadership. That said, though late in arriving, it was by no means a bad car. Stung by the experience of the Model K, Ford still was not prepared to consider a six-cylinder engine but, with a larger "four" than the old Model T, the attractive 3.3-litre Model A rapidly attracted around three hundred and fifty thousand advance orders. It sold well to begin with, too, and once word spread that Ford had "made a lady out of Lizzie"—that the country cousin had become the country club cousin—it chalked up a million sales within just sixteen months.

With four-wheel braking, a more conventional three-speed selector gearbox, and coil ignition, it was technically advanced by Ford standards. But it faced stiff competition. By now only Chrysler and the Dodge brothers were producing cars with less power than Ford, the blame for this being laid firmly at Henry Ford's door and an old man's adherence to engineering principles that were both anachronistic and inflexible. To begin with, its output was only 20 horsepower, but strenuous efforts were rapidly being made to wring more power from the block, and 40-horsepower models were soon available for sale to customers.

The new car was light, too. Ford recognized that "the more a car weighs, naturally the more fuel and lubricants are used in propelling it; the less weight, the lighter the expense of operation." Weight, he said, had nothing to do with strength, and his car was accordingly 500 pounds lighter than the rival Chrysler and nearly

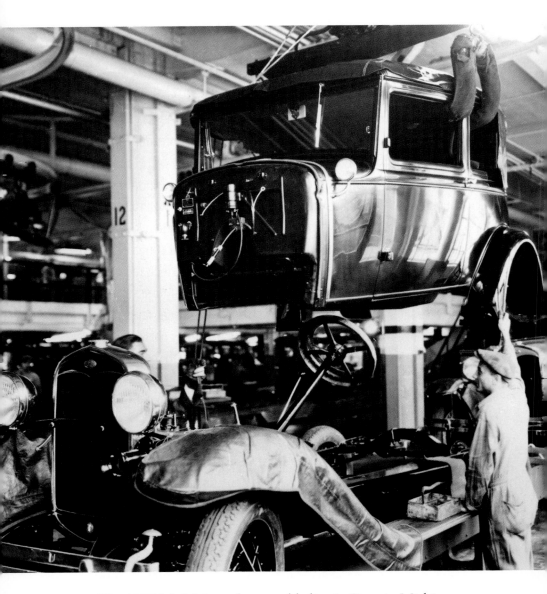

The 1927 Model A on the assembly line in Detroit, Michigan.

a thousand less than the smallest Buick. America's remaining auto manufacturers appeared committed to the concept of bigger is better.

Because it was light, the car was relatively fast and it also offered plenty of acceleration. More significantly, it was robust, reliable, and affordable—the virtues that had attracted buyers to the Model T and that were soon to put Ford back on top. Chevrolet may have trumped the blue oval in 1927 and 1928, but by 1929 the Ford Motor Company was back on form. Thanks to the Model A it was able to post half a million more registrations than its nearest rival while banking a handsome $91 million ($1.3 billion in 2016) profit.

Even Ford must have realized, however, that neither he nor his cars would ever again dominate the world as they had once done. The success of one manufacturer in toppling Henry Ford showed others that it was possible. Shorn of his apparent invincibility, he was soon facing repeated attacks from Chevrolet's parent, General Motors, and its intelligent, thoughtful head, Alfred P. Sloan.

A graduate of the prestigious Massachusetts Institute of Technology, Sloan differed in almost every regard from the backyard naturals like Ford, who had built up the auto industry in the early days. Where Ford ruled his company like it was his personal kingdom, basing key decisions on a mixture of instinct and his own homespun philosophy, Sloan had an educated, flexible mind and a more corporate outlook. Observing Ford, he saw that such large business entities could no longer rely simply on the hunches and gut feelings of a single individual.

Alfred Pritchard Sloan (1875–1966) was president of General Motors, a major competitor of the Ford Motor Company.

Dividing General Motors into semiautonomous divisions, and seeking to build "a car for every purse and purpose," it was Sloan who introduced the concept of annual model changes, which stood at such variance to Ford's own way of doing things. Fortunately for him, Ford had Edsel by his side, a man who, in his father's words, "knows style, how a car ought to look" and who responded by introducing annual styling changes to the Model A and its successors.

This helped but there were bigger problems on the horizon. In 1929 the Wall Street crash devastated manufacturing, throwing millions out of work and dramatically affecting new-car sales. Assuming the pain would be short-lived, Ford cut his prices sharply, but to little avail. His dealers simply went out of business or switched to other marques with bigger margins, and even an offer to increase his own workers' wages did nothing to halt sliding sales.

The country was soon swamped with second-hand cars and, with global production approximately halved by the slump, everyone was hit—none harder than Ford. Volume sales fell by two hundred and fifty thousand in 1930, and by five hundred thousand more in 1931 as the lead was once again surrendered to Chevrolet. In April of that year the company produced its twenty millionth car, but with the London *Times* reporting that it had also made an annual loss of £10 million ($45.5 million in 1931, approximately $721.4 million in 2015), fanfares were muted. Instead Ford struggled to think of something that could galvanize the market as the Model T had done all those years before—and revive his personal fortunes.

At Chevrolet, Sloan had successfully launched a new six-cylinder engine specifically to challenge the Model A's "four," and it was this that at last drew a response from Henry Ford. It came in the form of the world's first mass-produced **V8**, a timely move and the last great contribution the old man was to make to the industry that for so long had seemed his own.

Work on the 3.6-liter engine had actually begun in 1929, but Ford was far from happy with it initially and continued to insist that he had "no use for a motor which has more spark plugs than a cow has teats." Scale drawings were still rare in his world, and despite having more than a dozen well-equipped research laboratories, Ford liked to boast that the company did "nothing at all in what is sometimes ambitiously called research."

Personally he always preferred what he called "the Edison method of trial and error." To test whether pressed steel was stronger than forged he had Joe Galamb sit on a strip of each, declaring "that's all right" when the former was seen to bend the least. It worked for Henry Ford, and it seems charming today, but in an increasingly sophisticated industry such methods were beginning to look bizarre.

So, too, was Henry Ford's reliance on ever bigger four-cylinder engines, and when at last he changed his mind he admitted it was almost entirely down to Sloan and General Motors. Explaining to anyone who cared to listen, Ford would say, "we're going from a four to an eight, because Chevrolet is going to a six."

Insisting that "anything that can be drawn up can be cast," Ford was again determined to produce his new engine as a single

Henry Ford relied on his long-time employee József Galamb (1881–1955) to refine the technology behind his ideas, including Ford's mass-produced V8 engine.

cost-effective piece and once more turned to his old associates Galamb and Sorenson to make it happen. It took time but they did it, and, following its launch in March 1932, more than two hundred thousand V8-engined cars were shipped in the first year. An improved version appeared a year after that, and with none of his competitors able to offer such an engine at such a low price, Ford once again took the lead. In 1935 his company beat General Motors in both sales and profits.

But Henry Ford's new high was to be his last. The following year General Motors was back in the lead, and once again he found himself playing catch-up. In truth, it was Ford's tragedy that for much of this period his eye was off the ball. Distracted by labor issues, from 1936 onward he seemed increasingly to have spent more time worrying about the unions than deciding what to build.

Tough times had brought labor relations into sharper focus. More paranoid than ever, Ford bundled the unions up with the Jews, with Wall Street, and Franklin D. Roosevelt's New Deal to create what in his own eyes was a multifaceted, octopus-tentacled, all-purpose conspiracy to bring him down.

The United Auto Workers Union was a particular problem and, with the company's supervision of its workers proving more and more restrictive, Ford relied heavily on an ex-boxer named Harry Bennett to maintain order through a hand-picked team of bruisers and heavies.

Bennett's methods were so crude that workers at the giant Rouge River plant increasingly relied on what was termed the

"Ford Whisper," a means of talking without moving the lips in order to communicate covertly during working hours.

For Ford the unions were "the worst thing that have ever struck the earth because they take away a man's independence." His reasoning stemmed from a conviction that increased unionization was the child of big-city finance, that Wall Street wished only to entrap the workers. Refusing to acknowledge the passing of the 1935 National Labor Relations Act, he barred unions from his plants and continued to do so even when Chrysler and General Motors were moved to accept their terms. Anyone who did not like this found themselves facing Bennett and his bullies. This combination of physical brutality and sheer pigheadedness somehow enabled Ford to hold out until 1941.

In such a tough market, however, Ford could not survive like this for long. Had it not been for a second war with Germany, it is conceivable that the company might not have survived at all. The irony of this was not lost on observers: the company founded and run by the great pacifist and peacemaker now came to rely on weapons production to secure its future. Ford did not invent the jeep, but his company built more than two hundred and seventy-five thousand of them under license, together with trucks, tanks, and engines, before once again turning its attention to the efficient production of aircraft.

Now more than ever the forces arrayed against Germany and Japan needed to tap into Ford's production expertise. Work began immediately on a new $60 million ($967 million in 2016) assembly line at Willow Run, just outside Detroit. The world's

Male and female workers rivet the wing section of a Liberator bomber at Willow Run.

largest, at nearly a mile long, the end product was to be entire airplanes, not merely engines—thousands of them.

Built in higher numbers than any American type before or since, the airplane in question was the B-24 Liberator bomber. By 1944, the plant outside Detroit was running at such a high level of efficiency that a new one was being wheeled out on to the apron every hour. Eventually more than eighteen thousand of them were completed, and at a peak rate of around six hundred and fifty a month, Ford was building half of them. Confounding critics who had nicknamed the vast plant "Willit Run," such was the rate of production that pilots routinely bunked down at the plant, ready to take off the moment a new B-24 was cleared to go.

One of the machines that saved the Allies, the Liberator saved Ford as well. During the course of the war Ford plants built nearly eighty-seven thousand aircraft in all, more than four thousand military gliders and tens of thousands of aircraft engines, superchargers, and generators. Almost certainly no one other than Henry Ford could have done it, but against a background of falling car sales, one also has to ask what he might have done instead, had the military contracts not been there for him to sign.

10 Legacy

*The **Times** in London described him simply as "one of the world's most outstanding individuals." According to the same newspaper his principal achievement—bringing the car within reach of ordinary families—was "the greatest revolution of his day." Ford wasn't just making cars but remaking America.*

Notwithstanding the immense success of Willow Run, the war for Ford was overshadowed by the death of his son and heir in May 1943. Edsel Ford was only forty-nine when he died, bullied in life by his father, and in his

Crowds gather to attend Henry Ford's funeral on April 10, 1947, at St. Paul's Episcopal Cathedral in Detroit, Michigan.

Henry Ford (*center*) is joined by his grandson Henry Ford II (*left*) and his son, Edsel (*right*), at the Ford Motor Company exhibition for the New York World's Fair on April 5, 1939.

premature death just another victim of Ford's strange dietary fetishes. He died of cancer after contracting a fever brought on by drinking unpasteurized milk from the family farm, but the stress of working under such a strong, dictatorial figure as his father has long been assumed to be an additional, complicating factor.

Now in his eightieth year, Ford resumed the presidency of the company but he too was ailing, having suffered two strokes and then a third, apparently after being persuaded to watch film footage of the worst excesses of the Nazi persecution of European Jews. Alarmed at the possible implications for its largest domestic manufacturer—at this point also a critically important component of its war economy—the US administration discharged Edsel's son from his navy service and sent him home.

Back in Dearborn, twenty-five-year-old Henry Ford II assumed the role of company vice president, but the position was in name only. Overshadowed by his grandfather and bullied by Harry Bennett, any attempts he made at real change were swiftly thwarted. Fortunately he found some powerful allies, not just within government but inside the family, and when Edsel's widow and then Henry Ford's own wife threatened to sell their stock, Ford himself was finally persuaded to step down. He did so on September 21, 1945, Henry Ford II moving swiftly afterward to sack Bennett and his "gangster army."

The war was over. The company was in dire straits and hemorrhaging funds at a rate of well over $2 million ($26.4 million) a week. With one hundred and fifty thousand workers and around fifty plants in two dozen countries, it was still a powerful force, but by 1946 Ford's share of the domestic car market had slumped to 21 percent. On a turnover of $1.2 billion ($14.6 billion) it made a profit of barely $2,000 ($24,300 in 2016). Worse still, no one on the staff had any real idea of how much it actually cost to build a car, or where to begin when it came to the all-important

Spectators line the streets of Detroit to see the funeral procession for Henry Ford.

business of forecasting trends. Henry Ford, in other words, had left behind a mess: a ticking time bomb.

Despite having no background in the industry—on succeeding to his patrimony he told reporters, "I don't know enough to be frightened"—Ford's grandson nevertheless succeeded in turning things around with incredible speed. A year after he assumed control, profits were up to $65 million ($791 million in 2016), then $100 million ($985 million in 2016) in 1948, and nearly twice that the following year. In only three years he paved the way for the company, which has survived into the present day.

But for all Henry Ford II's achievements, it is his grandfather's legacy that most impresses today. Reporting his death on April 7, 1947, the *Times* in London described him simply as "one of the world's most outstanding individuals." According to the same newspaper, his principal achievement—bringing the car within reach of ordinary families—was "the greatest revolution of his day." It was a phrase that recognized that, with the Model T, Ford wasn't just making cars but remaking America.

Ford's death came only eighteen months after his retirement from the firm he founded, at a time when the company continued to insist he was in excellent health. He died, as he would have wanted, on his estate at Fair Lane, in suburban Dearborn, close to his birthplace. After his body was embalmed, a line nearly a mile long formed of neighbors and workers, past and present, keen to pay their respects or at least to see for themselves that a figure who had dominated America and American industry for so long had indeed passed on.

Success had come relatively late to Ford, but he had grasped it with both hands. Forty years old when he founded the company that still bears his name, and forty-five when he introduced the Model T, he was fifty by the time moving assembly lines and higher wages were in place, which would make his fortune and change the world forever.

Years later, in his groundbreaking television series *Civilisation*, Kenneth Clark observed that among the qualities that made the Dark Ages dark were "the isolation, the lack of mobility." Lacking Clark's education and erudition, Ford would have put it differently, but he saw the same truth with the same clarity. For him, the car was always much more than just a means of transport or an interesting technological challenge. It was a machine that could change the world, and his destiny was to make it happen.

In the 1890s, when Ford finished building his first Quadricycle, little consideration was given to the needs of automobilists. Motoring then was little more than an expensive recreation. In 1899, *Scientific American* carried an advertisement advising its readers to "dispense with a horse," but it took nearly a decade before this became a possibility for anyone but the richest and most adventurous. Not until 1908 and the Model T was it clear that these slow and noisy machines were going to have a profound impact on every town and city in the world and on the way people chose to live.

New York's Bronx River Parkway was the first highway expressly designed for the car's exclusive use, and it opened the same

Legendary innovator Henry Ford laid out at his funeral

year. With Ford's increasingly affordable Model T putting the world on wheels, the floodgates opened and cars were suddenly everywhere. More motorists meant louder demands for better roads, and after decades of ignoring the protests of carters, farmers, and cyclists, governments in the United States and elsewhere finally acknowledged the need for proper highways and started building them.

Of course, roads are only one aspect of the changes wrought, and progress has many masters. But it was Ford's imagination, drive, and sheer bloody-mindedness that made the car a reality for everyman. Carl Benz may have built the first, but he manufactured only a couple of dozen and was unable to visualize the almost limitless demand for them. Similarly, Ransom E. Olds may have been the first car maker to attempt mass production, but he fell far short of what Ford envisioned at Highland Park—and very far short of what Ford managed so quickly to achieve.

Ford's success also drove many other industries to new heights. A factory that consumed millions of billets of hickory wood (for wheel spokes) each year was music to the ears of timber producers. Similarly, a need for nearly half a million cow hides for upholstery provided a valuable income stream for the Chicago meat trade, as well as providing a neat payback for their earlier inspiration. Moreover, Ford's achievements were copied by rivals and admirers everywhere—among them Hitler and Stalin—and especially by leaders of other industries. Visiting Highland Park, or even just hearing about it, they began to grasp the immense potential of mass production. Using Ford's methods, they sought

VIEW ON THE BRONX RIVER PARKWAY

Ford's Model T was so accessible that car ownership exploded, resulting in the construction of highways, including the Bronx River Parkway, pictured here circa 1922.

to bring the lessons to bear on their own activities and often did so with almost equally spectacular results.

Ford's greatest power—appropriately for one of his background and lack of formal training—came from his belief in practical demonstration. At the 1906 Olympia motor show in London there were more than four hundred different cars on sale, ranging in price from £150 (US $727 worth $19,300 in 2015) to over £2,500 (US $12,125 worth $323,000 in 2015). Ford appeared and proposed selling his new four-cylinder Model N for just £125 (US $600 worth $16,000 in 2015), an announcement that was greeted with derision by local manufacturers who felt sure—or maybe just affected to believe—that nothing that cheap could be any good. Almost every company represented at that 1906 show is now defunct, but Ford soldiers on.

In later life Ford fancied himself as something of a philosopher. Besides his anti-Semitic tracts, he published several discursive books including *To-day and To-morrow* and *Moving Forward*. But he was no wordsmith and must have known he was at his best when showing-by-doing. Had he simply laid out the theory of how the car could change the world, still more how one particular model could conquer all, few would have believed him. But he didn't. From the earliest, Ford believed that "the market for a low-priced car is unlimited"—and then *showed* how it could be done.

The figures speak for themselves. When he launched the Ford Motor Company in 1903 there was approximately one car for every 1.5 million Americans. By the time Highland Park was getting into its stride, just five years later, there was one to every eight hundred. Not all of them were Model Ts and not all were Fords, but in time half came to be. Not even the VW Beetle was able to dominate the market in this same way, nor—while the baton of "World's Largest" continues to pass between Toyota and General Motors—will a single man ever again dominate the industry as Henry Ford once did. He was, quite simply, a giant.

Chronology

1863   Birth of Henry Ford

1879   Ford leaves home and begins working in factories, acquiring
expertise he will later put to good use

1888   Marries Clara Bryant and settles in Detroit, Michigan

1893   Birth of their first and only child, Edsel; makes his first
experimental gasoline engine

1896   In a backyard workshop Ford completes his first Quadricycle

1899   Resigns from the Edison Illuminating Company to cofound the
Detroit Automobile Company

1901   Detroit Automobile Company is dissolved; Ford establishes a
second company, the Henry Ford Company (later the Cadillac
Motor Car Company); goes racing and establishes numerous
national records

1902   Ford is forced out of the Henry Ford Company

1903   The Ford Motor Company is born; its first car is the Model A

1906   The company becomes the dominant manufacturer in the
United States, holding the position for twenty years

1908   The launch of the Model T

1910   Highland Park factory is opened, north of Dearborn

1911   Ford opens its first overseas plant, in Manchester, England

1913   Sales figures again increase dramatically, to more than
170,000 from just 68,000 barely two years earlier

1914 Ford more than doubles workers' wages to $5 a day

1915 Ford charters the "peace ship" *Oscar II*; its voyage to war-torn Europe is not a success; Ford's company builds its one millionth car

1918 Edsel becomes new company president

1919 A stock buyout means Ford controls 100 percent of the company

1920 Ford begins publishing overtly anti-Semitic material in the *Dearborn Independent*

1921 Ford Motor Company sells its five millionth car to become the dominant car company worldwide

1926 Diversifying into aviation, Ford becomes the first to mass-produce aircraft

1927 Ford finally gives in to the inevitable and closes the Model T assembly lines after building more than sixteen million cars; he closes the *Dearborn Independent*; Fordlandia in Brazil is acquired through a free land concession

1929 Wall Street crash

1931 Ford builds its twenty millionth car

1932 Ford launches the world's first mass-produced V8 engine

1933 Ford falls behind both General Motors and Chrysler

1935 Ford retakes the lead in both sales and profits

1936   Ford falls behind General Motors once more

1938   In the year he turns seventy-five, Ford receives a prestigious award from Adolf Hitler

1941   Despite his objections, the Ford Motor Company finally acknowledges the existence and legitimacy of the Union of Auto Workers; the company builds its first military jeep

1943   Death of Edsel Ford; Henry Ford assumes presidency of the company once more

1945   Ford is maneuvered out of the company by family shareholders and replaced by his grandson, Henry Ford II, who sells Fordlandia back to the Brazilians

1947   The death of Henry Ford

2014   An estimated one hundred thousand Model Ts are still thought to be running

Glossary

anti-Semitic Discriminating or hostile toward Jewish people.

assembly line A manufacture process in which products move through stages and operations in a line, such as by a conveyor belt, where workers or automated equipment perform the same operation for each product.

autocrat A person who rules with unlimited authority or influence, such as a monarch.

benefactor A person who helps others by donating money.

chassis For an automobile, the supporting frame on which the main parts are built.

cylinder A cylindrical chamber that is the core of an automobile engine, where the pressure of gas or liquid moves a sliding piston. Cars typically have four, six, or eight cylinders.

egomaniac A person who is thought to be excessively selfish, self-centered, or boastful.

epicyclic When an object moves in a circle, the center of which moves on another greater circle at the same time; also used to describe planetary motion.

flywheel A heavy wheel in a machine or engine that rotates on a shaft and controls the speed of the connected moving parts.

Fordism Named for Henry Ford's business practices, a manufacturing policy to constantly improve and maximize productivity and minimize cost by standardizing production through the use of assembly lines, deskilled labor, and uniform parts. This system of mass production brought economic growth in the United States after the world wars and empowered capitalism.

horsepower Measure of the power of an engine, particularly a car engine, and named for the force a single horse exerts. In the United States one horsepower equals 746 watts.

humanitarian A person who seeks to improve people's lives and who promotes human welfare and social reform.

industrialist Leader or manager of an industry, devoted to mechanization rather than agriculture, craftsmanship, or trade.

magneto An alternator that uses magnets to generate the current for the ignition in an internal combustion engine.

marque A make of a product, such as a car.

mass-market Describes products produced and distributed on a large scale to be sold to a wide range of customers.

mass production Products manufactured in large quantities, usually by machinery.

metallurgy The science of working with and manipulating metal into desired shapes, properties, and alloys.

mogul An important, powerful, or influential person, particularly of an industry or arena.

pacifist A person who is strenuously and actively opposed to conflict or war.

standardize To establish or make things similar and consistent according to rules, principles, or features. In production, to manufacture parts of the same size, weight, quality, strength, and material for near-identical assembly.

trade union (labor union) Organization formed by workers to protect their interests and rights, particularly as it concerns wages, benefits, and working conditions.

utilitarian Having the qualities of usefulness rather than beauty or luxury.

vanadium steel A steel alloy containing vanadium, making it lighter and stronger.

V8 A car or engine with eight cylinders, two sets of four set at an angle to form a V.

Further Information

Books

Bak, Richard. *Henry and Edsel: The Creation of the Ford Empire.* Hoboken, NJ: John Wiley & Sons, 2003.

Baldwin, Neil. *Henry Ford and the Jews: The Mass Production of Hate.* New York: PublicAffairs, 2001.

Barrow, Heather B. *Henry Ford's Plan for the American Suburb: Dearborn and Detroit.* DeKalb, IL: NIU Press, 2015.

Evans, Harold. *They Made America: From the Steam Engine to the Search Engine.* New York: Little, Brown & Co., 2004.

Ford, Henry. *My Life and Work.* Garden City, NY: Doubleday, 1922.

Grandin, Greg. *Fordlandia: The Rise & Fall of Henry Ford's Forgotten Jungle City.* London, England: Icon Books Ltd, 2009.

Setright, L.J.K. *Drive On!: A Social History of the Motor Car.* London, England: Granta, 2004.

Snow, Richard. *I Invented the Modern Age: The Rise of Henry Ford.* New York: Scribner, 2013.

Swigger, Jessie. *"History Is Bunk": Assembling the Past at Henry Ford's Greenwich Village.* Amherst, MA: University of Massachusetts Press, 2014.

Watts, Steven. *The People's Tycoon: Henry Ford and the American Century.* New York: A.A. Knopf, 2006.

Websites

American Experience: Henry Ford

http://www.pbs.org/wgbh/americanexperience/films/henryford/

The PBS history series *American Experience* has several videos on Henry Ford's rise from farm boy to innovator and father of the automobile. The main episode highlights how Ford's mission to mass-market the automobile changed our world.

The Henry Ford

www.thehenryford.org

This website will connect you to attractions, including pages for the Henry Ford Museum, Rogue Factory Tour, and research center, and resources, such as historical collections and primary documents.

Henry Ford Biography

www.biography.com/people/henry-ford-9298747

The Bio website has a video biography on Henry Ford with quick facts, detailing the span of his life, the Ford Company, and his controversial viewpoints.

The Henry Ford Heritage Association

www.hfha.org

Hosted by a historical association dedicated to Henry Ford, this website has information about Ford's life and lists events, museum exhibits, and talks on the historical figure.

Bibliography

Brinkley, Douglas. *Wheels for the World: Henry Ford, His Company, and a Century of Progress*. New York: Penguin, 2004.

Cole, Wayne S. *America First: The Battle Against Intervention, 1940–41*. Madison, WI: University of Wisconsin Press, 1953.

Cycle & Automobile Trade Journal. Philadelphia: Chilton Co.

Ford, Henry, ed. *Dearborn Independent*. Dearborn, MI: Suburban Pub. Co.

Ford, Henry. *My Life and Work*. Garden City, NY: Doubleday, 1922.

Grandin, Greg, *Fordlandia: The Rise & Fall of Henry Ford's Forgotten Jungle City*. London, England: Icon Books Ltd, 2009.

Lacey, Robert. *Ford: The Men and the Machine*. New York: Little, Brown & Co., 1986.

Setright, Leonard. *Drive On!: A Social History of the Motor Car*. London, England: Granta Books, 2004.

Sloan, Alfred P. *My Years with General Motors*. John McDonald, ed. New York: Doubleday, 1964.

Thacker, Tony. *'32 Ford: The Deuce*. Oxford, England: Osprey, 1984.

United States Office of the Coordinator of Inter-American Affairs. *The Amazon Awakens*. Film. Walt Disney Productions, 1944.

Index

Page numbers in **boldface** are illustrations. Entries in **boldface** are glossary terms.

Aerocar, 43–44
Agnelli, Giovanni, 7
Ainsley, Charles, 25
anti-Semitic, 87–91, 121, 128
Arrow, 32–34, **34**
assembly line, 7, 68–69, 71–73, 115–116, 124
Austin, Herbert, 17
autocrat, 6, 8

benefactor, 9, 76
Bennett, Harry, 114–115, 121
Bentley, Walter Owen, 8
Benz, Carl, 6–7, 25, 126
Bronx River Parkway, 124, **127**
Bugatti, Ettore, 8
Buick, 109

Cadillac, 31, 38
car, invention of, 6–7, 126
chassis, 15, 55, 59

Chevrolet, 69, 94, 109, 111–112
Chrysler, 107, 115
Citroën, 7, 68
cylinder, 25, 28, 38, 41, 44, 55, 58, 83–84, 107, 112

Daimler-Benz, 53
Dearborn Independent, 9, 85, 86–87, 89–90
Detroit, 8, 22, 31, 64, 65, 76, 115–116
Detroit Automobile Company, 29–30
Disney, Walt, 98
Dodge, John and Horace, 41, 107

Edison, Thomas Alva, 22, 23, 25, 29, 96
Edison Illuminating Company, 22, 25, 33
egomaniac, 8
epicyclic gearbox, 39, 57

Ferrari, Enzo, 8
Firestone, Harvey, 96